18

COPING
WITH COLLEGE

P9-DHZ-232

McGRAW-HILL COMMUNICATION SKILLS SERIES

Dr. Alton L. Raygor, Consulting Editor

Spelling
Lewick-Wallace: SPELLING

Vocabulary
Lewick-Wallace: VOCABULARY BUILDING AND WORD STUDY

Writing
Lewick-Wallace: PUNCTUATION AND MECHANICS

Future publication: GRAMMAR AND SENTENCE STRUCTURE

Reading
Future publications: READING FOR COMPREHENSION

IMPROVING READING RATES

Study Skills
Kagan: COPING WITH COLLEGE: The Efficient Learner

EDITOR'S INTRODUCTION

This book is one of a series designed to improve the basic skills of students in colleges and other educational institutions. Study skills, along with reading, spelling, vocabulary, and writing skills, have an important influence on school success. They must all be given separate, special attention.

The main focus of this book is on the improvement of study skills. Students will find that it is not a set of rules that must be followed or a lot of moralistic sermons. It is a solid, research-based work written in an easy style with many highly practical, specific suggestions for using study time more effectively.

The author, Corin Kagan, has a wealth of experience working with students of all ages, and is especially attuned to the needs and problems of the older student. She presents reliable, useful information that can be immediately applied to student life.

The book is very complete, well organized, and useful to students. The explanations and examples are clear and well written. It is an excellent book by a very competent teacher on an important topic.

ALTON L. RAYGOR
Consulting Editor
University of Minnesota

CORIN E. KAGAN
Normandale Community College

McGRAW-HILL BOOK COMPANY
New York | St. Louis | San Francisco
Auckland | Bogotá | Hamburg
Johannesburg | London | Madrid
Mexico | Montreal | New Delhi
Panama | Paris | São Paulo
Singapore | Sydney | Tokyo | Toronto

COPING WITH COLLEGE: THE EFFICIENT LEARNER

TO MY
husband, daughter, parents, friends, colleagues, and students

by whom I have been taught,
to whom I have been a teacher

because learning is a never-ending chain

**COPING WITH COLLEGE:
THE EFFICIENT LEARNER**

   34567890 DODO 8987654

ISBN 0-07-033191-X

This book was set in Megaron Light by Graphic Technique, Inc.
The editors were Phillip A. Butcher and David Dunham;
the designer was Nicholas Krenitsky;
the production supervisor was Diane Renda.
R. R. Donnelley & Sons Company was printer and binder.

Library of Congress Cataloging in Publication Data

Kagan, Corin E.
    Coping with college.

    (McGraw-Hill communication skills series)
    Includes index.
    1. College student orientation—Handbooks,
manuals, etc.   2. Study, Method of—Handbooks,
manuals, etc.   I. Title.   II. Series.
LB2343.3.K33   378'.1702812   81-14311
ISBN 0-07-033191-X   AACR2

CONTENTS

PART III THE EFFICIENT LEARNER: SPECIFIC CONTENT STUDY SKILLS

CHAPTER 10
STUDYING THE SOCIAL SCIENCES

CHAPTER 11
STUDYING SCIENCE

CHAPTER 12
STUDYING MATH

PART IV   A FEW FINAL WORDS AND AN ASSESSMENT

CHAPTER 13
CONCENTRATING ON THE TASK   **253**

CHAPTER 14
LOOKING BACKWARD AND FORWARD   **263**

PREFACE

Coping with College is written for a variety of student populations. Although the book is part of a series for two- and four-year college students, it is also suitable for high school students considering college, adults contemplating a return to school, and those enrolled in nontraditional programs.

The content is based on sound principles extrapolated from the empirical research data of learning psychology. It is written in a readable style—with the aim of imparting useful skills and information necessary for academic success. The student should be urged to try out and adapt the techniques rather than be "preached to" that these *are* the techniques. In other words, the book should be used as a tool, not as a cure-all.

The author assumes a reader who, although probably a student for at least twelve years, feels that his or her skills associated with academic success need upgrading or improving—a reader who is a busy, mature, multi-roled individual, engaged in a variety of life tasks in addition to that of being a student. *Coping with College*, therefore, attempts to focus on the psychological as well as the technical needs in skills knowledge for just such persons.

The chapters are arranged in a logical sequence for the purpose of building the skills needed to produce a sound study system. Each skill can be learned or taught as a separate unit depending on the needs of the student. As a whole, however, the skills constitute an efficient, effective package to assist the student toward academic success.

Coping with College contains skills illustrations, examples from a variety of subject areas, and exercises relevant to the major reading and study problems students encounter. These include time planning, listening and note-taking, text reading and retention strategies, preparation for and taking examinations, term papers and other college writing tasks, and using the library. In addition the book contains many special features, including a hands-on library exercise, a diagnostic arithmetic test, a self-help test anxiety exercise, illustrations of the major types of writing patterns and specific study strategies for science, social science, and math courses, and timetables for college writing assignments.

The student should be urged to complete the practice exercises and to apply them to course material. Indeed, supplementary practice exercises can be drawn from the student's own course needs as well as **xiii** from a variety of work texts stressing specific skills already in print and contained in most college libraries and/or learning centers.

To make *Coping with College* most useful, it is suggested that:

—Whether used as a course text or as the basis of an individual project, it is best to work through the book in its entirety and in sequence to gain the benefit from the organizational structure of the book.
—Students presently enrolled in college classes should be urged to begin with an evaluation of the elements of their classes to assist them in devising an efficient study plan as well as to guide them in determining the areas on which to put special emphasis while going through the book.
—The self-assessment at the beginning of each chapter should be done carefully. From the self-knowledge gained of one's strengths and weaknesses, the student can formulate goals for the reading, studying, and applying of each chapter in order to make the experience the most efficient, effective possible. It has been found that small group work within the larger framework of the study skills class (or the study skills support group within the framework of the skills center) is an effective technique. Discussion plus the sharing of goal setting with peers works well toward the achievement of academic skill goals.
—Each student should be urged to adapt or adjust any suggestion to meet individual academic and personal demands.

The organization of this book and the material included in it have been composed based on fourteen years' experience in classroom teaching and individual assistance to students in both two- and four-year colleges. While every student may not need intensive practice in each skill area, most students, especially those new to college or those just back in college after a lengthy absence, will find the information enlightening and useful in their bid to cope with academic life and to become the most efficient, effective student possible.

Corin E. Kagan

TO THE STUDENT

Since you have already been a student for at least twelve years of your life, maybe you're wondering why you are now enrolled in a study skills course, or at least why you are reading this book. Just being a student does not mean that you know how to study.

If you are like most students, you want to do well in college. After all, you freely chose to come to college, and most likely you are paying for it yourself by working or you have worked and saved for many years to get an education. You also realize that it is going to be a different experience from any previous schooling you ever had.

For some of you, school has not been a good experience. Whether you continued directly from high school or returned after a long absence, you may wonder why you are here and how you can make it a good experience. Since motivation is a key to success, you may wonder how you will make it through in light of a less than positive attitude toward your classes. Some of you have always enjoyed school and now want to make it even better. Others have been out of the classroom for a long time. While coming back to school was your choice, representing a big step in your life, you feel that your motivation and will to succeed are strong.

That brings us to *study skills*—what they are and what they can do for you.

I can begin by telling you what they are not. No matter how much previous schooling you have had, study skills are not automatic. They don't come with the territory. Study skills are not a set of ideas or rules dreamed up by people to confuse you or make school more difficult.

Study skills have their basis in psychology, specifically the psychology of learning. The ideas come from experimental and clinical evidence that demonstrates how people learn best.

Study skills are a set of habits that develop over time. Like all habits, they can be either good or bad and also can be changed or improved upon.

Study skills are teachable, learnable techniques that can help make getting an education an efficient, high-quality, pleasurable experience. They enable the student to plan study time efficiently. Knowing what has to be accomplished when you hit the books usually means getting the most out of a study session in terms of achieving the best grades possible. After all, although school is a priority in most students' lives, many students also work at least twenty hours a week and have family, friends, and social demands eating away at their time.

Whatever you do in life, the skills of effective listening, good note-taking, and efficient reading and time management are essential. In school, at work, or in the community, it is necessary to listen to and process information. You need the skill of being a good listener in a lecture hall at college. But it is equally important in a meeting chaired by a colleague or the boss, as well as in a political or social action group on the community level.

Time management is essential for the student and vital for the worker for whom deadlines are important and usually not so clearly defined as in college. Discipline is required regardless of whether the due date is six months away for a report or sales quota on the job, or six weeks away for a paper or exam in a college course. Good work and study habits learned in one situation are also useful in other situations in our lives.

Sound good? It should.

Till now, any study skills you may have learned along the way have probably come in a hit-and-miss fashion. If you did learn some in a school experience years ago, they have been forgotten or you have neglected to practice them. The material in this book has been planned to give you a systematic, practical approach to success in studying. Each skill will be taught with the idea of its practical application to your life as a student. It will be up to you to apply what you learn in this class and in your other courses.

You may feel that you know this stuff or that you need to learn the skills taught in the middle of the book more than the ones at the beginning or end. Be patient. It has been the experience of most students in classes such as yours that a complete review is helpful. It is just as important to review what you do know as what you don't know. After all, one does not tackle a mountain or an open body of water without first being taught the techniques of skiing or swimming and then practicing them on hills or in a swimming pool. A skier or swimmer practices by training, building up skills and confidence. Success at each succeeding step marks a point on a line leading toward an ultimate goal: becoming the most efficient, effective skier or swimmer around. So it is with students and study skills. First you have to know yourself and your needs as a student. Then you will learn the techniques and skills in those areas that will increase your chances of success as a student. Apply them in your courses. Consistent practice and the will to succeed usually constitute a strong combination which can ultimately lead to your development as an efficient, effective student.

This book should be read in sequence, from the opening chapters that deal with an assessment of both yourself and your study tasks through the general and then the more specific study skills chapters, ending up with an assessment of what you have learned and what you still need to accomplish. However, for many students, concentration is a factor in school success. Although it is discussed at the end of the book, anyone wanting to read Chapter 13 sooner should do so. It is probably best to read it after Chapter 3, Planning for the Task: Time Management.

Corin E. Kagan

STARTING OUT:
WHAT IT TAKES TO
GET DOWN TO WORK

I

LOOKING AT YOURSELF

This chapter is concerned with who you are as a student and a person. It describes active and passive learners, attitudes toward change, and some common problems of students. It then goes on to present material which suggests ideas for investigating the school, the curriculum, and yourself to assist in a better understanding of yourself as a learner.

Think about yourself as a student in your previous experiences with education and as a person in your relationships, career plans, feelings, and attitudes. Write down some of the thoughts that come to mind.

As a student, I _____

_____

_____

As a person, I _____

_____

_____

Therefore, in reading this chapter, some of the information to which I want to pay particular attention is _____

_____

_____

YOURSELF AS A STUDENT

Most of this book is about you as a student, and so it deals with the skills necessary for being at your best in an academic setting. This section is going to be about you as a person. It's true that the two are closely connected; your image of yourself is reflected in your actions as a student. However, for a little while let us concentrate on the person behind the student.

Consider first, What made you decide to come to college? Write down all the reasons that come to mind.

_____

_____

_____

Some of the most frequent answers to that question are:

- It was the most logical place to go after high school.
- It was the first step in finding myself after being a homemaker for twenty years.
- It means that I can earn a better living in the future.
- It's a stepping stone for a career.
- It means being able to do anything I want in the future.
- It represents the acquisition of an education.

The last answer is by far the most common one.

Now let's explore what the term "education" means to you. Write down what being educated represents to you.

_____

_____

Some of the most frequent answers to that question are:

- It means independence in life.
- It means being able to do anything I want in life.
- It means the acquisition of a better job, leading to more earning power.
- It means learning.

The last answer is by far the most common one.

Let's go one step further and explore what the term "learning" means to you. Write down what learning represents to you.

_____

_____

Some of the most frequent answers to that question are:

- It means knowing information.

- It means greater understanding.

- It means knowledge.

- It means opening broader horizons.

Obviously these terms, which mean different things to different people, represent various possibilities and personal philosophies. Whatever terms you use, the basic concept remains: Education implies learning, and learning implies a learner, or a student.

ACTIVE VERSUS PASSIVE STUDENTS

The kind of student you are (or have been or will continue to be) arises directly from your perception of yourself. An active or passive person gets translated into an active or passive student.

What are active people? Active people are self-motivated, independent, and responsible for themselves and their actions; they question authority when appropriate, either to gain information or to assert their rights.

Active students, therefore, participate in their own education, leaving little or nothing to chance or to any other person. Active students are independent learners, doing assignments thoroughly and on time. This sometimes means going beyond the assignment—reading more or extra material when the subject is interesting or when there is a need to know more in order to be able to comprehend better. Active students ask questions in class or seek outside help from instructors or friends when the subject matter is unclear or difficult.

What are passive people? Passive people are controlled by others rather than by themselves. They are quick to blame others for their problems, aim to please others rather than themselves, and do not question authority or assert their rights when appropriate.

Passive students, therefore, do not participate in their own education but instead are the victims of instructors and/or the "system," who are usually held responsible for the problems related to being a student. Passive students procrastinate on assignments and usually will not do any more than what is assigned. Passive students do not raise questions in class or visit instructors to gain information or clarification when assignments are difficult or unclear.

Learning is an active process in which you become involved with the education you want for yourself. This means selecting the courses and programs you need to become an "educated" person, including perhaps a basic math or English course to upgrade deficient skills, as well as the courses and programs you need to fulfill career or personal goals.

Active learning implies hard work and change: change in the way things are done and change in habits and outlook. Active learning involves personal change. This involves risk, and risk-taking is scary. For example, it means giving up procrastination, which, if not satisfying, is certainly safe. Being responsible for your own education means doing things in a way that pleases you, producing growth in you as a person. Sometimes that growth startles or confounds those around you. Change in you implies that others also have to change to accommodate new aspects of your behavior and personality. An active person knows that change occurs over time, as a result of new information or acceptance of new attitudes or opinions. This may mean bending significant other people out of shape and changing relationships, or possibly even ending them.

Active learning implies an active learner—an active learner is an active person.

EVALUATE YOURSELF AS A LEARNER

Read each statement and answer according to the scale on the right.

	Never true for me	Sometimes true for me	Undecided	Always true for me
I ask questions in class.	_____	_____	_____	_____
I seek out the instructor to get information or clarification on points I do not understand.	_____	_____	_____	_____
I read beyond the assignment when the subject interests me.	_____	_____	_____	_____

I complete all assignments thoroughly and on time.	_____	_____	_____	_____
I feel that the instructor knows what's best for the student.	_____	_____	_____	_____
I feel put upon when more than one instructor makes heavy assign-ment or test demands at the same time.	_____	_____	_____	_____
My getting good grades is import-ant to my family.	_____	_____	_____	_____
I sometimes wonder why I am in college.	_____	_____	_____	_____
I am probably not as intelligent as the other students in my classes.	_____	_____	_____	_____

CHANGE

In the preceding section on active people and learning, the word "change" was used frequently. In this context, it implies variety, newness, risk, challenge, time, caution, resistance, and, at its worst, impossibility. Familiar ways are just that—old, unvaried, comfortable, safe, and usually repetitious. Nobody ever grew very much, as a person or a student, without change.

Reflect on your feelings about change and the ideas about it you have heard expressed by others. Some common statements about change include "I can't change," "It will take forever to change," and "I'm too old to change."

Let's look at some of the assumptions behind these statements. The statement "I can't change" implies impossibility. The speaker assumes a rigid posture and resists anything new. Using the word "can't" alongside "change" implies no choice at all on the part of the speaker. The speaker is saying, "This is the way I am, this is the way I always will be, and there's nothing I can do about it." Nonsense and irrational. All people can change themselves or their study habits to the degree that they choose to change. You may not be able to change because you don't know how, but that does not imply that you can't. In most cases it involves just a lack of knowledge of how to do it. Think of all the places you use the word "can't"—"I 'can't' do math," "I 'can't' swim." What are some of your "I can'ts"?

Look at each statement and try to figure out the reasoning behind it. Take "I can't swim," for example. Is it because you never learned, or learned improperly, or because you fear the water as a result of a bad experience you had? Perhaps you don't swim because you hate to get your hair wet, or any one of a dozen other reasons. Unless you are handicapped in such a way that you can't take care of yourself freely and, therefore, can't go into a body of water alone, you are able to swim if you so desire. In other words, you can. Unless you have a problem beyond your physical or mental control, you *choose* not to swim. That's your prerogative, your free choice not to do something. So instead of saying "I can't swim," say "I won't swim." Look at your "I can't" list and replace "can't" with "won't."

Some feel that it is impossible to change because of the time involved, thinking that change takes forever. That is up to you. No one ever changed overnight, or changed completely, but change is possible over time. The question is, How important is it to you to change a habit or an attitude that is holding you back from getting where you want to go? If it is important, it's worth the time and effort. If fear has been keeping you from the desired end of learning to swim, you have to invest time and effort to change your attitude and behavior. It will mean seeking out a good instructor, attending the lessons regularly, and practicing till you reach a comfortable level of proficiency. It takes time and effort. No one ever promised that change, or life for that matter, is easy.

Older students frequently reject change because they fear that their age is against them; older folks are not supposed to be able to learn, because they are too set in their ways. Nonsense. Anyone can learn at any age. Occasionally older students have to give themselves a little more time to grasp ideas, especially if they have been away from the classroom and formal learning for some time. Old dogs do learn new tricks. They can change their habits. Besides, older students have the experience of years of living to bring to any new situation.

Another statement you hear often is, "That's me. I am that way, and I can't change." Nonsense. No one is molded out of stone. Change is possible if you want to change. You may never have written in a book, and so learning to underline may seem like a sacrilegious thing to do. If you want to learn this skill, because the benefits that accrue to the student from having a variety of study techniques are invaluable, then you can. Writing in books may not be comfortable at first. From firsthand evidence and experience, you can see how useful a tool it is for a student. Little by little, over time, you change.

For as long as there have been students, there have been thoughts and problems plaguing them. Some have been consistent over time; others are new and depend upon the social and economic stresses of the times.

YOU AND YOUR COLLEGE CLASSMATES

One meets a mixture of students in higher education. In high school, at home, or even in the business world, the tendency is to associate with people much like ourselves—people who think and feel and act in a way that is comfortable and familiar to us.

College is a mixture of people with attitudes, ideas, and values as varied as their numbers. People from cultures never before encountered may appear strange or perhaps even threatening. People with different ways of life or different moral or ethical standards speak and act in alien ways. In a sense, this experience in higher education is a microcosm of society, a cross section of what the world is really like as opposed to the insulated part of the world in which we tend to live.

For the person from a small town, however, it is a chance to meet people from the city. For the businessperson, it is a chance to get in touch with the younger generation. For the returning student, it's a chance to get back in touch with all kinds of people and ideas. For any person, it is a chance to get to know, understand, and learn to accept people with different points of view, philosophies of life, and moral and ethical standards.

The ups and downs of our society—the economics, politics, and social fabric—always present problems to students. Whether times are good and jobs are plentiful or times are bad and jobs are scarce, students are always torn between work and school. In good times there is money to be made, and school may not seem necessary for success. In bad times, money is needed to survive, but education seems to be the path to success. The ever-present question is, Do I really need a degree in today's world?

There have always been students who doubt their intelligence or ability to complete a college program. Higher education represents a greater cross section of learners than a student has ever encountered before. Students fresh from high school are confronted by students from high schools all over the state and even the country. Students fresh from years at home or in the business world are confronted by students who are younger and therefore closer to the school experience than themselves. In either case, the new situation represents competition and increased anxiety.

In some cases, younger students realize that they may not be as good students as they once believed or as high school grades may have led them to believe. Compared with high school, college competition is on a broader scale. College classes have students from all over the city, state, or country. For other students, abilities and skills are reaffirmed as being good or above average.

Older students generally feel anxious and inferior to younger students. However, most instructors who have adults in the classroom find this a misconception. If you are an older student, be assured that although you may look different from your younger counterparts in age or clothes or may be different in values or breadth of experience, in no way are you less capable than someone half your age. If anything, those differences give you an edge in the learning process. Older students are just as capable of learning as younger students and in some cases even more able.

Regardless of your age, if you have freely chosen to get an education, welcome. No one ever said that every day of your life would be easy. Some days at college will test you severely. If you are trying out the idea of education to see how it "feels," welcome. Decisions are based on information and evaluation. You'll never know unless you try it. Knowing whether you belong and knowing your potential are searching processes. You must give yourself every opportunity to investigate the school, the curriculum, and yourself in order to make effective decisions.

INVESTIGATE THE SCHOOL

Whether you are attending or planning to attend a two- or four-year college or a vocational technical school, and regardless of whether you plan to work for a degree or only complete one or more courses of your choosing, to be fully involved you must know your school and what it can offer. Too many students attend classes and then head for home or work. While it is true that students lead busy lives as workers, homemakers, parents, friends, and relatives in addition to their involvement in education, a school's services are usually varied enough to relate to many, if not all, the roles played by a person.

The Faculty

The faculty of an educational institution is usually its greatest asset. Take time to get to know the instructors. In many areas they have not only academic knowledge but practical experience that is yours to share. Most teachers in professional programs such as nursing, business, drafting, and computer technology have worked or still work actively in the field. They are potential sources of information about the job market as well as good advisers on curriculum choices. In most cases, instructors are people who like to talk about their subject areas and experiences. Take advantage of their posted office hours or invite them to join you for a cup of coffee. Too often students think of instructors as being superhuman, knowing everything, and being above it all. It's just not true. They enjoy the common pleasures of life and have problems just as you do. Get to know your instructors. It makes education a lot more fun.

Student Support Services

In addition to the faculty, the student services division of your school is a virtual treasure-house of support and information. Student services usually offers both personal counseling and academic advising. In many schools, an appointment with a counselor or adviser is required before registration for the next term, especially if you have not yet declared a major and your choice of course work is unclear. Even if you have selected an area of concentration, frequently checking in for academic advising ensures that you are taking the proper courses in sequence and have the requisite number of credits toward graduation.

Frequently, the people who do academic advising also do personal counseling. In some schools, these services are provided by two different sets of people. In any case, it is not uncommon for students to need to talk over an issue that is bothering them—anything from indecision over career choice to a troubling relationship or a severe depression. It is neither shameful nor wrong to seek out a neutral ear. If the school has such a service and you need it, use it. If your school does not offer personal counseling, an academic adviser usually can refer you to a community agency that will supply the needed help.

Student services divisions usually have financial aid advisers—people who know the what, where, when, and how of obtaining money to finance an education. They know which scholarships or loans are available, the necessary qualifications, when to apply, how to fill out an application, rules for repayment of loans, etc. Frequently associated with this office is a job-finding (and sometimes even a job-placement) service. The service consists of lists of jobs, both on and off campus, full-time as well as part-time.

Job placement is sometimes done for students who are completing a professional program. For example, students majoring in such areas as business, medical technology, nursing, and secretarial services are registered with and hired through the school's placement office just before or upon graduation. In some cases, the placement service is ongoing even after graduation. Another service of a placement bureau is to keep your records, recommendations, and references on file. They are sent to potential employers at your request. This process is ongoing and continues long after graduation.

Most schools provide a social and intellectual outlet for students in the form of a college center or student activities program. Organizations as diverse as college government, school newspapers and magazines, athletic facilities and intramural teams, camera or boating clubs, and music, theater, and debate groups offer a variety of ways to get involved in the school. Many schools also run an arts program, scheduling concerts, plays, movies, and even trips at a reasonable cost. Many schools have clubs for special interest groups such as returning students. This is a wonderful opportunity to meet people much like yourself; to share ideas, problems, and solutions; and to build a support network of friends. If you are new at school, meeting and talking with others like yourself is a great way to feel comfortable fast. Older students tend to keep to themselves till they realize that they are accepted by the younger students. They need to meet others in the same situation. Even after an older student breaks through to the younger students, it is still good to have peers for company in classes, in car pools, or to share a cup of coffee.

Included in the services of most schools is a learning or skills development center. In some institutions it is part of student services; in others it operates through a specific discipline, such as English. In some instances it is an independent operation. Whatever its nature, it represents a place where you can go to upgrade academic skills such as reading, note-taking, underlining, spelling, grammar, and math. Learning centers offer individually programmed courses on a credit or noncredit basis, small-group workshops in such areas as math and test anxiety or reading efficiency, and term-long courses for credit in reading and/or study skills. Many centers provide tutoring services in math, science, and other academic disciplines, and some offer assistance in proofreading themes and term papers. If your school has a learning center, investigate its services and use it. Learning center personnel are among the most helpful people you'll find on campus.

Most schools have a student handbook that describes the many services offered. Take the time to read it carefully. You'll probably find an office or program that will help you find the answers to all your questions about the school.

As part of a learning center, or sometimes separately, many schools are now equipping career resource centers. These are highly specialized libraries containing all types of information to assist students in making career decisions. Sometimes a counselor or faculty member will suggest you visit the center to read about particular careers or a general area of interest. Many schools offer a course in career exploration, and assignments are made in the career center to acquaint you with its material and how it can serve you in the decision-making process.

INVESTIGATE THE CURRICULUM

Just as there is a handbook of student services, there is usually a book describing the curriculum as well as the rules and regulations of the school. It is usually known as the bulletin or catalog. Frequently, student services information is contained within the catalog.

Catalogs or bulletins list and describe all the courses offered in the curriculum. The course description gives the general purpose of a class and the major topics covered. Also included is the number of credits the course is worth, prerequisites if there are any, and how many times during the year the course is offered.

The bulletin also lists the degrees or certificates the school awards and the requirements for completing each program. This includes both the general school requirements and the specific requisites for each professional program or degree.

Bulletins also describe the special learning opportunities available to students, such as chances to earn credit and/or experience beyond the normal classroom opportunity. These might include:

- Cooperative education programs, in which you work at a job in an area you are considering for a career or as part of your chosen major. While earning anywhere from 3 to 15 credits a term, you will be getting firsthand experience working at the career of your choice or in a job that may lead you to make or reject a career choice.

- Independent study programs, in which you design a course of your own to go beyond classroom learning. This can mean coming up with any reasonable set of learning goals, planning and negotiating their accomplishment with an appropriate faculty member, and carrying them out on your own. Your purpose may be to read about and investigate an area just touched on in a course you enjoyed, or to work on an area about which you've always been curious, or to check out an area you are considering for a career.

- Competency-based education, in which you receive credit for your life experiences and design projects and select appropriate courses to fashion your own degree program. Students returning to school with extensive volunteer or business experience frequently find this a fine way to earn credit for their life's work and to get the necessary education to augment their experiences in order to get a meaningful degree.

The bulletin also contains rules and regulations regarding scholastic achievement. This includes the grade-point average you will have to maintain to remain in the school or in a particular program, the conditions of academic probation, what you must do to enter into or change to another curriculum, and the definition of such concepts as withdrawal from a course, an incomplete grade, and auditing a course. It is best for you to read your school's catalog and become familiar with the rules and regulations of academic survival.

Regarding grades, the catalog will usually tell you the value of each letter grade and how to compute your grade-point average. In most schools, the system is as follows:

A = 4 points

B = 3 points

C = 2 points

D = 1 point

To compute your grade-point average, multiply the grade-point value by the number of credits. Add up the total grade points and divide by the number of credits. For example, suppose one term you had psychology (5 credits), advertising (4 credits), physical education (1 credit), and study skills (3 credits), for which you received grades of B, D, C, and A, respectively. Using the grade-point values assigned above, compute your grade-point average.

COURSE	LETTER GRADE	GRADE-POINT VALUE	CREDITS	GRADE POINTS
Psychology				
Advertising				
Physical education				
Study skills				

Grade-point average = _____

The answer is at the end of the chapter.

A word about an incomplete grade. Sometimes circumstances prevent you from completing the assignments in a class or taking all or some of the tests. Obviously, this situation should be avoided whenever possible. If it does become a reality, an incomplete grade is one way to save the course grade from becoming a failure or keep yourself from having to withdraw from the course or school. If you want to negotiate an incomplete, see the instructor immediately and propose an alternative plan for completing the work or making up an exam. In most schools, courses must be completed by the end of the next term. Read the catalog for the rules and regulations of your institution. Incomplete grades are not desirable; they represent an unfinished task and interfere with the work of the next term. But they represent an option so long as you use them wisely.

Occasionally students withdraw from a class rather than accept a failing grade. This is necessary when an incomplete is not feasible. However, many students withdraw without consulting the instructor. All too often the student who withdraws was doing better than he or she thought. I have heard instructors say that they were holding papers or tests with above-average grades from students who withdrew from a class without consulting the instructor. Although a withdrawal can be necessary, it is suggested that you don't use this option hastily, or unwisely, or without consulting the course instructor.

Rules and regulations vary from school to school. Learn your school's policies on incompletes and withdrawals.

INVESTIGATE YOURSELF

The idea behind this chapter is that you are a choice-maker. The choices relate to you and what you will do with your life. This obviously goes beyond the kind of student you choose to be, extending to your whole person: how you will interact with others, what kind of intimate relationships you want, what career you will select, how you want to spend your free time, and how you perceive yourself. These are only a few of the many areas in which you have a choice. However, many people never realize that they have such freedom; they never take advantage of their choices because they don't know themselves well enough to make the appropriate choices.

The following exercises will help you begin the process of thinking about and looking at yourself. In no way do they represent a complete overview. Self-exploration is a lifetime project. From time to time, all people need to stop and take stock of themselves—where they are at the moment and where they want to go. To make it less of a game of chance, self-exploration is the place to start. Many schools offer courses or small-group experiences in personal exploration. They are a good way to self-inspect, meet other people in your institution who are eager to do the same thing, and earn some credits, all at the same time.

Exploring Yourself—Now

—Physically, I would describe myself as _____

_____

_____

—Intellectually, I would describe myself as _____

_____

_____

—Emotionally, I would describe myself as _____

_____

_____

—The things I like best about myself are: _____

_____

_____

—The things I like least about myself are: _____

_____

_____

—The things I do best are: _____

_____

_____

—The things I do worst are: _____

_____

_____

—The most important goal in my life is to _____

_____

_____

—My other goals are: _____

_____

_____

—In the last five years, I've changed in the following ways: _____

_____

_____

—In the next five years, I'd like to change in the following ways: _____

_____

_____ _____

Exploring Yourself—The Past

—What do you remember being told, either in words or in nonverbal messages, by your parents, teachers, and friends about:

—your abilities as a student _____

_____

_____

—the meaning of work _____

_____

_____

—your own sexuality _____

_____

_____

—displaying emotions such as love, anger, and sorrow _____

_____

_____

—death _____

_____

_____

—people who appear different from yourself _____

_____

_____

—values (loyalty, achievement, justice, power, morality, and religious faith) _____

_____

_____

Exploring Yourself—The Future

—When I think about the future, I see _____

_____

_____

—Some of the important decisions I have to make in the near future involve my

—educational plans (selecting a major, going on for more schooling,

etc.) _____

_____

_____

—career plans (in choosing a career, the most important considera-

tions I have are) _____

_____

_____

—personal values (values I would like to strive to achieve are) _____

_____

_____

—personal goals (during the next five years, ten years, twenty-five

years, I would like to accomplish the following) _____

_____

_____

—interpersonal relationships (I would like to increase my ability to interact with my family, mate, friends, work colleagues in the

following ways) _____

_____

_____

Take a minute and reread your responses to the questions about your present, past, and future. Now write a summary paragraph describing the person depicted in those statements: the ideas, attitudes, goals, values, and perceptions of yourself you may have; where they came from in your past; and your plans for the future.

Answer to grade-point average problem:

COURSE	LETTER GRADE	GRADE-POINT VALUE	CREDITS	GRADE POINTS
Psychology	B	3	5	15
Advertising	D	1	4	4
Physical education	C	2	1	2
Study skills	A	4	3	12

Total = 13   into Total = 33

Grade-point average = 2.5

SUMMARY

—What you do and how you perform as a student are determined partly by what you think of yourself as a person and a student.

—This determination is made from the messages you get from your experiences, your family, your friends, and the school itself.

—Although change involves risk, change is possible if a person wants to change.

—Higher education is different from all your previous school experiences. It can be either an opportunity to expand mentally and socially or a repeat of previous experiences.

—To get the most from any educational experience, you need to be aware of what the school has to offer and what the curriculum has to offer and put that together with investigating yourself to find out who you are and where you want to fit in.

LOOKING AT YOUR CLASSES | 2

This chapter is a personal investigation of the elements that go into any college class: the instructor, the textbook, the lectures, the notes you take during lectures, the exams, and the papers you write. A brief personal assessment in each area is followed by some short statements on the subject. The aim of the chapter is to have you evaluate yourself and your classes in each of these areas and then use the information for planning study strategies.

Mentally review your study habits and attitudes in each of the areas mentioned above (relationship to instructors, textbooks, lectures, note-taking, exams, and writing papers).

In which areas do you feel that you do well? List the areas and the habits you have that contribute to your success.

As a student, I believe I do well at _____

_____

_____

_____

In which areas do you feel you do poorly? List the areas and the habits you have that do not contribute to your success.

As a student, I believe I do poorly at _____

_____

_____

_____

Therefore, to get the most out of this chapter, the information you will want

to pay particular attention to is _____

_____

_____

_____

In this chapter you are going to consider the basic elements of college classes: the people who teach the courses you take, the texts you read, the lectures you hear, the notes you take at those lectures, the tests you take, and the papers you write. It will take you the better part of the first week of a new term to find out what is happening in each of your classes and plan strategies for the successful completion of each course and its assignments.

Be alert and observant during the first class sessions. Listen carefully to the instructor's directions and read the syllabus carefully to gather information for the questionnaires that appear in this chapter. As you are observing and recording the information, go on to the next section of the book, returning to do the analysis at the end of the first week of the term. However, you must read the chapter and each questionnaire before gathering the data so that you will know the kinds of information you are looking for.

Each section contains general statements about its subject. You will have to think about yourself and your relation to the subject in general and to your courses in particular. Read the statements and respond to them. This will give you a chance to assess your strengths and weaknesses. It will allow you to see the areas to be strengthened by improving techniques and by practice. Try to determine what you feel are the causes of some of your study problems.

In addition to filling out the questionnaires for each course, it will be good for you to record your reactions or impressions of your classes as you attend them for the first few days of a new quarter or semester. By doing this, you can get in touch with the ups and downs of college life, your attitudes toward the course and instructor, the boredom, the anger, and the disagreements and disappointments, as well as the successes and positive feelings you get in relation to your classes and study techniques. Keep a diary in a notebook, jotting down your feelings and thoughts at the end of each day of classes. It is another method you can use to determine how well this book can work for you and in what areas you may need more help.

Each questionnaire will be followed by information on its topic. Read it carefully.

Finally, you will be asked to analyze your classes in order to discover the meaning of the information you have gathered. The relationship of the basic elements of all college classes will tell you what is expected of you in a particular class. Although you may not be able to see it now, this experience will point the way toward the development of a study system for each class and the use of the general and specific study skills techniques you will read about in this book.

Once you have completed all the questionnaires and readings, you are ready to evaluate the information and make preliminary plans for getting down to work.

Using the information you gathered and recorded on the questionnaires, fill in the chart on page 38. Be as specific as possible.

For each course, write down what you learned about the specific area (the instructor, the text, the lecture, etc.) and yourself in relation to that area. For example, you may have learned that the text is the basis of the exams as well as the lectures in a course. The instructor covers about three chapters each week. You should have an idea of the difficulty level of the book as well as knowledge about your reading ability in relation to the assigned task. All this information adds up to your study strategy for that particular course. Therefore, you may decide that it is wisest to read small sections of the book at a time, taking notes as you go in order to be adequately prepared for both the lectures and the exams.

Or you may have learned that a particular course is going to be more difficult than you imagined, with several short themes assigned over the course of the term. Since writing may not be one of your favorite tasks, your study strategy for that particular course will be to begin those assignments early and get them done well before the deadline so that they will not interfere with other course assignments.

You may find that you have a lecturer who speaks quickly and is poorly organized. Although you feel you are a good note-taker, you foresee problems getting everything down on paper. Therefore, plan to read the text carefully before each class lecture and go over your notes each day after class with a friend, comparing them to make sure you each got all the material in your notes.

To sum it up:

1. Read through the entire chapter first.

2. Gather the information you need from your classes and yourself to fill in the questionnaires.

3. Fill in the questionnaires.

4. Using the information, plan your study strategies for each course on the Class Analysis Form at the end of the chapter.

5. Review your analysis from time to time when conditions in your courses change or when you feel that the strategies you planned are not working well for you.

THE PEOPLE WHO TEACH THE COURSES YOU TAKE

Who are the people who teach the courses you are taking? Probably they are people with a strong commitment to teaching, a good knowledge of the subject matter, and in the case of instructors in occupational programs, people with extensive firsthand experience in the field.

Whoever they are, there are some things for you to think about in regard to the instructors and their teaching behaviors, which can be used to your advantage in your learning.

Most instructors have a plan in mind when they begin a course. They know the subject matter, and they know what aspects of it they want the class to learn, and by what method.

This plan is not a mystery for you to solve by yourself; most instructors reveal it when they present the course syllabus at the first class meeting. Depending on its completeness, the syllabus shows such things as the order of presentation of the subject matter, the nature of the course assignments, whether they are reading or writing assignments or both, when they are due, the number of exams and when they will be given, and the grading system.

Study the syllabus. Note all the due dates for assignments and tests and immediately jot them down on your master calendar (more about that later).

If you are in a course that does not have a syllabus, the responsibility for getting the information by asking direct questions of the instructor is yours.

From the assignments, you can also get an idea of what knowledge or background it is assumed you have brought to the class. In most introductory or survey courses, little or no prior knowledge is assumed. However, in more advanced classes, it will be assumed that you know the basic concepts and vocabulary. In some science courses and in each successive math course you take, it is assumed that you have the knowledge to continue your study of the subject.

Your instructors' classroom behavior reveals their enthusiasm for the subject and the nature of the desired classroom interaction. Some instructors lecture for the whole class period. Others give information but encourage discussion between teacher and student, or student and student, that leads to a sharing of diverse points of view.

You will want to find out about the accessibility of your instructors— how willing they are to help you outside of class. Find out when the instructors hold office hours. Most instructors want students to come around and ask questions about work as well as discuss ideas stimulated by the course content. This kind of responsible student behavior is one of the main differences between high school and college; it makes for a person who is a lifelong learner.

The people who teach the courses you take are only one element in your success in college. A person who is enthusiastic, who is a stimulant to a student's interest, motivation, and thinking, and who is available to help the student outside class is always an aid to learning. However, if you

THE PEOPLE WHO TEACH THE COURSES YOU TAKE

FILL IN THE NAMES OF
YOUR COURSES

	Course 1	Course 2	Course 3

EVALUATE THE INSTRUCTOR
(Fill in each box with the appropriate answer.)
The instructor:
—Makes the course plan clear

—Presents the material in a clear, organized way

—Stimulates student interest, motivation, and thinking

—Is enthusiastic about the subject matter

—Is interested in helping students

—Encourages lively class interaction

—Assigns easy/difficult reading material

—Asks less/more of students than they can do

EVALUATE YOUR ATTITUDE TOWARD THE INSTRUCTOR
(Answer yes or no to each statement for each course you are taking.)
—I understand what is wanted by the instructor in this course.

—I enjoy going to class.

—I feel comfortable going to see the instructor to ask for help or exchange ideas.

—I feel that I am being motivated to do my best work.

—I feel that I must motivate myself in this course.

—I feel that the instructor is willing to help students.

don't happen to run into a superteacher in every course you take, the responsibility falls on you. It will mean turning off negative thoughts about the subject matter, the instructor, or both. You will have to motivate yourself to succeed in that class. We'll say more about that later on.

THE TEXTS YOU READ

However the text is used, there are certain basic considerations to take into account in your approach to studying.

First, there is the book itself. Most texts are written with the student in mind and contain a variety of study aids. Chapters are usually divided by major headings, and each major section is usually broken down into important subcategories. This will help you follow the author's plan in writing as well as organize the material for learning purposes. Frequently an outline of the ideas presented will appear at the beginning of the chapter, and more often a summary of the ideas contained in the chapter will appear at the end. Many text authors include study questions for you to answer or sample problems for you to work out. Important vocabulary can be italicized or set in bold print or in print of another color. Glossaries, or dictionaries of terms important to a subject, are placed at the end of each chapter or at the end of the book. Standard book features such as the table of contents and index should not be overlooked as study aids.

The second consideration is you. Before reading any text, you must consider your basic reading ability, what you know about the subject, and the way you usually handle a text.

What is the status of your general reading skill? The efficient reader has a variety of reading speeds, reading rapidly for general ideas and slowly to note details. The efficient reader has an extensive vocabulary and the ability to locate and use an author's structure.

Before reading a text, you must consider your background or previous experience with the subject matter. If you have had an introductory course in the subject in high school or in your previous college experience, you can expect to at least recognize some of the vocabulary and ideas in the new text. On the other hand, if the subject is entirely new, both the concepts and the vocabulary will be unfamiliar. In math, which is a cumulative subject, you can expect to recognize terms, ideas, and processes in each succeeding course. In psychology, anthropology, or economics, you will probably spend more time familiarizing yourself with the specific vocabulary and ideas that the author presents, because they are new to you.

What do we mean by being able to handle a text? It refers to having a purpose for reading, knowing what it is both you and your instructor want you to know each time you sit down to do some reading. This implies a systematic approach to text reading. It means reading for a purpose, not

THE TEXTS YOU READ

FILL IN THE NAMES OF
YOUR COURSES

	Course 1	Course 2	Course 3
EVALUATE THE TEXT (Fill in each box with the appropriate answer.) The text is used: —as the basis of the lecture			
—in addition to the lecture			
—independently of the lecture			
The text contains aids for studying: —subdivided headings			
—chapter outlines			
—summaries			
—problems			
—study questions			
—glossaries			
The concepts and vocabulary in the text are/are not totally new to me.			
My background in this subject area is limited, adequate, good.			
EVALUATE YOUR TEXT READING: (Answer yes or no to the statements for each course you are taking.) 1. I believe my general reading skills are good/poor.			
2. I can read rapidly for ideas.			
3. I can read slowly to get meaning and note details.			
4. I survey the material before reading.			
5. I know what information to get from the text before starting to read.			
6. I know what information the instructor wants me to get from the text.			

FILL IN THE NAMES OF
YOUR COURSES

	Course 1	Course 2	Course 3
7. I review right after I read.			
8. I have a variety of techniques for remembering what I read.			
9. I know how to schedule my time for reading.			
10. I know the importance of the text in relation to the exam.			
11. I am satisfied/not satisfied with my text-reading strategy for this course.			

reading for as long as you can stand it before you stop. It means having a variety of techniques for remembering what it is you read: underlining, outlining, mapping, and charting. It means knowing how to schedule your time for reading in a particular course so that you don't fall behind.

THE LECTURES YOU HEAR

The lectures you hear in college will vary, depending upon the person who presents them and the nature of the subject matter.

Some instructors prefer to use a prepared speech. This approach usually makes it easy to follow the structure of what is being said. Some instructors put an outline of the lecture topic on the board or provide one in the syllabus. This makes listening easier. Some instructors prefer to speak off the cuff. Although they may know what they intend to cover in a lecture, the discovery of the structure will be up to you.

Since course elements are tied together, you will have to determine the relationship between the other elements and the content of the lecture.

For example, what is the relationship between the text and the lecture? Sometimes the text and the lecture cover almost exactly the same ground. Sometimes the lecture is on the same subject as the reading assignment but goes far beyond it, giving additional material from the instructor's wide reading or experiential background. Sometimes the lecture ignores the text altogether and covers material not included in the course content but thought to be important to it. Here the lecturer often draws on a wide and varied background to help you learn.

You must also be aware of what the lecturer is doing with the course material. Is the lecturer's purpose to explain the course material, illustrate

THE LECTURES YOU HEAR

	FILL IN THE NAMES OF YOUR COURSES		
	Course 1	Course 2	Course 3
EVALUATE THE LECTURES: (Fill in each box with the appropriate answer.) Are the lectures given from: —a prepared speech so that I can follow the structure			
—from an outline on the board or syllabus			
—off the cuff so that I have to discover the structure			
Does the content of the lecture: —follow the text			
—supplement the text			
—ignore the text			
The purpose of the lecture is to: —explain the course material			
—expand on it			
—illustrate it			
—demonstrate an application of it			
EVALUATE YOUR LISTENING: (Answer yes or no to the statements for each course you are taking.) 1. I am usually aware of the structure of the lecture.			
2. I am usually aware of the lecturer's purpose.			
3. I am aware of the relationship between the lecture and text.			
4. I can recognize when the lecturer is saying something important.			
5. I have a hard time following the lecturer because:			

FILL IN THE NAMES OF
YOUR COURSES

	Course 1	Course 2	Course 3
—I have negative feelings about the lecturer			
—I have difficulty with the subject matter			
—I am unprepared when I go to class			
—I have so many other things on my mind			
6. I am satisfied with my listening skills in this class.			

or expand on it with examples or case studies, or demonstrate the application of the subject matter?

As a student in a typical class, you will spend about 45 percent of your time listening, as opposed to reading, writing, or talking. The ability to listen well and recognize the structure of what is being heard depends partly on intelligence and partly on willingness to listen. If you attend a lecture and are not prepared for the day's work, claim to be easily bored by the subject matter, or constantly express negative feelings for the lecturer, you may as well have cotton in your ears, because you are not allowing the lecturer or the subject matter to get through to you.

More on listening when we get to Chapter 4.

THE NOTES YOU TAKE

The notes you take will depend on the style and content of the lecture material.

If the lecturer is well-organized, your job as a note-taker will be easier, because the main points and supporting details will be clearly laid out for you to follow. In this situation, you will probably be able to take notes in an outline format. If the lecturer speaks off the cuff, making the organization a little harder to follow, your notes will probably reflect this and be less systematic. It will be necessary for you to make order out of the chaos, preferably right after the class session. More about this in Chapter 4.

The notes you take will also be influenced by the relationship between the text and the lecture. If both are quite similar, you will probably take fewer notes than if the content of the lecture supplements or completely ignores the text.

Your notes will also reflect the lecturer's purpose in speaking. In math or biology, for example, you will want to note examples of the process involved in problem solving or a biological chain of events such as photosynthesis. In a law enforcement or nursing class, your notes should reflect case studies and practical procedures used in dealing with the public, whether they are lawbreakers or patients. In history, your notes should reflect the relationship between cause and effect in the evaluation of historical events.

The most important feature of the notes you take is their "usability," or how useful they will be for studying purposes. This involves having a systematic approach to note-taking, going over your notes after each lecture, and the method you use for remembering the information for testing purposes.

THE NOTES YOU TAKE

	FILL IN THE NAMES OF YOUR COURSES		
	Course 1	Course 2	Course 3
EVALUATE THE NOTES: (Fill in each box with the appropriate answer.) The class requires notes that are: —reflections of the text			
—supplements of the text			
—further explanations, demonstrations, or applications of the text			
The amount of notes taken in a lecture for this course should be: —a great deal			
—a moderate amount			
—varied, depending on the topic			
EVALUATE YOUR NOTE-TAKING: (Answer yes or no to the statements for each course you are taking.) 1. My notes are poor because: —the lecturer goes too fast			
—the lecturer is very disorganized			

	Course 1	Course 2	Course 3
—I don't know what is important			
—I don't have a good system for note-taking			
—I don't go over my notes regularly			
—I have trouble paying attention in class			
2. My notes are difficult to read for study purposes.			
3. I don't know how to remember the notes I take.			
4. I know how important the notes are in relation to the exam.			
5. I am satisfied with my note-taking in this class.			

THE EXAMS YOU TAKE

Instructors give tests for a variety of reasons. It is one way to evaluate a student's work and assign a grade. It is just as important for an instructor to know how well the course material has come across to you. Therefore, a test will tell the instructor how well and how much you have understood.

You may not believe it, but tests, and especially tests given frequently, are great motivators. They force you to study and give you a way to evaluate your progress. Most people will argue that tests are not perfect measuring instruments, but they are widely used and are a fact of college life. You may run into some alternative, experimental method of evaluation, such as competency-based criteria for learning, but for the most part testing will be a part of your college experience.

Most college courses have at least two major exams—a midquarter or midterm and a final. Some final exams cover all the material from the beginning of the course; others cover only the material from the time of the midquarter. If you are not told what will be covered, you must ask the instructor well in advance of the test to allow yourself adequate time to prepare.

In some courses, especially math and science, there are quizzes every other week (or sometimes every week). Occasionally a quiz may be sprung on you to keep you on your toes. Again, let me stress that this isn't

THE EXAMS YOU TAKE

	FILL IN THE NAMES OF YOUR COURSES		
	Course 1	Course 2	Course 3
EVALUATE THE EXAMS: (Fill in each box with the appropriate answer.) The exam will be: —multiple choice			
—essay or short answer			
—problem solving or lab experiments			
—application of information			
—a combination of the above			
There will be (number of exams)			
Frequency of exams (weekly, etc.)			
Nature of the exams: —regular quizzes			
—midterm			
—final			
—a combination of the above			
Weight of the exam in relation to course grade:			
EVALUATE YOUR EXAM STRATEGY: (Answer yes or no to the statements for each course you are taking.) 1. I am unsure how to study for an exam in this course.			
2. My background in this course is poor.			
3. I predict sample questions while I am studying.			
4. When I study, I write down topics that I believe will be on the test.			
5. I review frequently during the term.			

	FILL IN THE NAMES OF YOUR COURSES		
	Course 1	Course 2	Course 3
6. I cram at the last minute.			
7. I read over the whole exam before beginning it.			
8. I outline questions on essays before answering them.			
9. I panic when an exam is announced.			
10. I panic when I take a test.			
11. I never do as well on a test as I thought I did when I was taking it.			
12. I have trouble taking the kind of exams given in this class.			
13. I know how much of the grade is determined by the exam.			
14. I feel that my exam-preparation and exam-taking strategies are good.			

done out of nastiness but to keep you motivated in your studies. It is done in your best interests. Honest!

What kinds of tests can you expect? Some classes lend themselves to subjective or essay-type exams. These are tests in which you must respond to a question by recalling information and putting it in your own words in a few well-organized paragraphs. Subjective exams are common in history, sociology, and humanities courses.

Some classes lend themselves to objective or multiple-choice exams (or possibly true-false or fill-in-the-blanks exams). These are tests in which you recognize the information and make a distinction between correct and incorrect information. Objective exams are common in science classes but also are popular in social sciences and humanities classes.

Some classes lend themselves to problem-solving exams. These are tests in which you have to apply the knowledge gained in a course to a specific situation. Problem-solving exams are common in science courses such as chemistry, biology, and physics; nursing courses; and math courses.

There are other types of tests, however, such as open-book tests, take-home tests, and oral tests. Open-book tests are usually subjective in nature. They are not as easy as you may think; unless the information in the book is known very well, you will spend more time searching than writing the answers. Take-home tests are usually open-book tests. The problem here is limiting both the time spent on the test and the amount of material included in the answers. Oral tests are common in foreign language classes and oral communications classes.

THE PAPERS YOU WRITE

Not every course you take will require a written paper. Virtually none are required in basic math or science courses. But you can expect weekly writing assignments in most introductory English courses and at least three to four papers in more advanced ones.

It is reasonable to expect a writing assignment in most academic courses, such as sociology, history, psychology, geography, and literature or the humanities. The same is true in many occupational programs, with papers usually required in the more advanced courses, such as business management, sales, marketing, nutrition, and human services.

The kind of paper you will be asked to write will depend on the nature of the subject matter and the person teaching the course.

In basic English courses, the papers will usually be brief and will give you practice in applying the writing techniques being taught in the course. In more advanced English courses, the paper will usually be longer. It will also call for you to demonstrate your knowledge and ability to apply writing techniques. It is in these classes that you will probably be taught how to write both themes and term papers. The difference is that the content for the former comes from your head, the latter from outside sources.

In content-oriented courses, it is unusual for more than one paper to be required. The instructor will usually tell you the required length of the paper and when it will be due and frequently will select the subject matter.

It is not uncommon, however, for you to have a lot of freedom in choosing a subject, with the instructor giving only a general idea of what is wanted. Research papers of this type rarely exceed ten pages in length. What is always required, however, is a reporting of the topic in an intelligent manner, with well-documented evidence to support your ideas, all presented in a literate manner that indicates your ability to use the mechanics of the English language properly.

THE PAPERS YOU WRITE

	FILL IN THE NAMES OF YOUR COURSES		
	Course 1	Course 2	Course 3
EVALUATE THE PAPER REQUIREMENTS: (Fill in each box with the appropriate answer.) Papers to write in this course			
Type of paper: —research			
—theme			
—book report			
Length of paper:			
Subject matter: —given by instructor			
—freedom of choice			
Due date:			
EVALUATE YOUR PAPER-WRITING SKILLS: (Answer yes or no to the statements for each course you are taking.) 1. I have never written a research paper, theme, or book report.			
2. I usually don't know what to write about.			
3. I have difficulty selecting a subject.			
4. I do not know how to use a library to collect information.			
5. I have trouble organizing information once it is collected.			
6. I do not know the proper format for: —bibliography			
—footnotes			
—the final draft of the paper			

FILL IN THE NAMES OF
YOUR COURSES

Course 1	Course 2	Course 3

7. I usually wind up writing a paper at the last minute.

8. I have trouble with the mechanics of writing:
   —spelling

   —grammar

   —punctuation

9. I believe that my paper-writing techniques are good.

CLASS ANALYSIS FORM

(To be filled in after completing questionnaires and reviewing your answers.)

The Basic Elements	Course 1	Course 2	Course 3
The texts you read (from reading and analysis, I gathered the following information)			
The person who teaches the class (from observing and analysis, I gathered the following information)			
The lectures they give (from listening and analysis, I gathered the following information)			
The notes you take (from taking and rereading my notes, I gathered the following information)			
The tests you take (from taking or preparing for a test, I gathered the following information)			
The papers you write (from writing or planning to write a paper, I gathered the following information)			
The unknowns (things I do not as yet know about the course but must find out)			
Study strategies (to succeed in this course, it would be best if I used the following study plan)			

PLANNING FOR THE TASK: TIME MANAGEMENT

3

This chapter is concerned with time: how it is spent and misspent. It starts with an analysis of how you spend your time, followed by a step-by-step plan for making a time schedule.

Mentally review how you plan and use your time. Complete the following statements:

I use time _____

_____

_____

The things that get in the way of my using time wisely are _____

_____

_____

_____

In relation to time, I do my best work when _____

_____

_____

_____

My feelings about time planning are:

    It is a waste of time ____ I don't know how to do it ____

    It never works for me ____

    Other comments: _____

_____

_____

_____

Therefore, based on your thinking and your responses to the above statements, the information you will want to pay particular attention to in this chapter will be concerned with _____

_____

_____

_____

Our perception of time is a strange thing. Most of us believe that we either don't have enough time or have too much. Either way, the work we want to accomplish—whether it is homework, housework, or having fun—never gets completed. If that statement describes you or thoughts you have had at any time, did you ever stop to think why this is so?

Time mismanagement is usually the result of setting unrealistic goals: planning to do too much in too little time, not planning enough to do in the time available, or not planning at all. In any case, lack of self-awareness and of the actual time you have available, as well as lack of knowledge regarding the planning, creating, and maintaining of a time schedule, contributes to illusions about time.

In addition, most people tend to confuse priorities by working on tasks of lesser importance first or doing pleasant chores before unpleasant ones. Some people find it difficult to say no to anyone or anything and wind up letting their time be planned by others rather than by themselves. Others let the unexpected take over, and both their time and their lives become victims of fate.

If you have no idea of where your time goes—that is, whether you truly don't have the time available or are wasting the time you do have—you might begin by trying the following exercise. Using the chart provided, list your activities and accomplishments as specifically as possible for each hour of the day for an entire week. For example, for time spent studying, list not only the hours but the number of pages read or problems solved. This information will help you plan a schedule when you get to the next section of this chapter. Be sure to include your work, home, and social commitments as well as the chores you do regularly, such as shopping and talking on the phone. If you spend time napping or goofing off, be sure to list that as well.

If you are reading this book on your own, go ahead with some of the later chapters while you are filling in your "portable conscience." You may want to cut the following Time Analysis Chart out of the book, duplicate it, or write your own on a separate piece of paper. Carry it around with you (the portable part). Record all your activities (the conscience part). Feel free to alter the hours listed on the side if you live by a different time clock. Many students do their sleeping during the day, working and taking classes at night.

At the end of the week, find some quiet time, review the week, and use the information from the chart to answer the questions in the Time Analysis Form.

You may not want to follow yourself around all week. You will, however, want to analyze the way you spend your time and learn how to plan and stick to a schedule. Proceed to the section headed Time Analysis.

Time Analysis for week of _____

	Mon.	Tues.	Wed.	Thurs.	Fri.	Sat.	Sun.
7 A.M.							
8 A.M.							
9 A.M.							
10 A.M.							
11 A.M.							
12 –							
1 P.M.							
2 P.M.							
3 P.M.							
4 P.M.							
5 P.M.							
6 P.M.							
7 P.M.							
8 P.M.							
9 P.M.							
10 P.M.							
11 P.M.							
12 –							
1 A.M.							

TIME ANALYSIS FORM

How do you spend your time?
What percentage of the week do you spend on:

Homework and studying	_____	percent
Family and home obligations	_____	percent
Work	_____	percent
Friends and social obligations	_____	percent
Goofing off	_____	percent
The unexpected	_____	percent

When you do an assignment:	Course 1	Course 2	Course 3
How long does it take?			
How many pages do you generally read in an hour?			
How many problems do you solve in an hour?			

What activities or tasks could be shared or carried out by another member of your family or by a roommate?

_____

_____

_____

What activities or tasks listed on the analysis could be eliminated?

_____

_____

_____

How is the way you are spending your time related to your routine goals? (In other words, if school is a priority, are you spending enough time studying?)

_____

_____

_____

How would you like to spend your time?
What percentage of your time each week would you like to spend on:

Homework and studying   _____ percent
Family and home obligations   _____ percent
Work   _____ percent
Friends and social obligations   _____ percent
Goofing off   _____ percent
The unexpected   _____ percent

What are the consequences of continuing your present time-use pattern on:

The courses you are presently taking? _____

_____

_____

The courses you intend (or need) to take in the future?

_____

_____

_____

What are some actions you could take to accomplish this change?

Take fewer courses _____   Rearrange your priorities _____
Eliminate unnecessary   Say no more often _____
tasks _____   Give up school(work) _____
Share work or get others to
do more around the house or
apartment _____
Learn how to make and stick
to a time schedule _____

Your ideas _____

_____

_____

Select at least one action that you would like to work on in order to change

the way you use your time. _____
What steps would you have to take to accomplish this goal?

_____

What benefits would you derive from accomplishing this goal?

_____

Summarize what you learned from doing this exercise.

_____

_____

TIME-PLANNING

If you are a new college student, just out of high school, you probably have not been in the habit of making a time schedule. You have not seen a need to plan your time, since up to now all your schoolwork has been accomplished during the regular school day.

If you are a new student to college, and especially if you have been at home (or on the job) during the past few years, you probably have been in the habit of making a schedule or at least a "to do" list to accomplish all the tasks that fill your day. Since you may feel you already know how to plan, doing your homework should just be a matter of fitting it in or adding it on to your other chores and obligations. This isn't necessarily true, nor will it necessarily work.

There is a need to learn how to time-plan, since the major portion of your college work will be done outside the classroom, on your own.

Planning, or determining how much time you have, what you have to do, and how you will do it, involves decision making. Good decisions necessitate gathering information and then using the information for making and following through on the plans and revising them if need be, based on the feedback you are getting. The steps that follow will teach you that process.

Step 1: How Much Time Do You Actually Have?

Using the Fixed Hours Schedule, fill in all the fixed hours in your day. These are times when you have regular obligations that are not changeable. They include hours you are in class and hours you are at work or have home or family obligations such as meal preparation. Be sure to include things such as sports, music or choir practice, or other social or volunteer activities that you do on a regular basis. If your job hours vary on a weekly basis, you may want to duplicate the chart and put in your work hours weekly. For most students, however, making a schedule of fixed commitments need be done only once, at the beginning of the school term. You should now be able to see the time you actually have available for studying purposes.

Step 2: What Do You Have to Do?

The next step is to list all the things you must do, both in the coming week and in the coming term. Since your assignments vary, making a weekly list allows time-planning to be a flexible activity. Let's begin with the long-range assignments. For each of your courses, list the nondaily assignments and due dates during the coming term: tests, projects, speeches, etc.

Long-range assignments such as these usually wind up being done hastily at the last minute. Aside from the fact that they are not done to the

	Mon.	Tues.	Wed.	Thurs.	Fri.	Sat.	Sun.
7 A.M.							
8 A.M.							
9 A.M.							
10 A.M.							
11 A.M.							
12 –							
1 P.M.							
2 P.M.							
3 P.M.							
4 P.M.							
5 P.M.							
6 P.M.							
7 P.M.							
8 P.M.							
9 P.M.							
10 P.M.							
11 P.M.							
12 –							
1 A.M.							

Fixed-hours schedule

TO DO LIST: Week of _____ 198_

TO DO

Accounting
Read Ch. 4, 20
pages, and work
3 problems.
Due: 5 days

Study Skills
Read Ch. 7 & 8,
40 pages, edit
one set lecture
notes. Underline
chapter to hand
in. Due: 3 days.

English
Read Ch. on parts
of speech (10
pages), make note
cards.
Do exercise end
of chapter.
Test on parts.
Due: 1 week

See Cslr. about
major choice.

Shop for birthday
present for
PM party

Get tickets for
Saturday game

Take Joe to work
Thursday after-
noon

student's (or teacher's) satisfaction, several days of concentrated work usually puts you behind in all your classes. The end result is that you are constantly playing a game of catch up.

Your long-range list should also include social plans or other obligations during the coming term which will force you to take time away from planned study activity.

Next, work on a weekly basis. For each of your classes, list the work that must be accomplished during the coming week. Be very complete, including the number of pages to be read, problems to be solved, assignments to be written, notes to be gone over, and vocabulary to be learned. Also list other school activities, such as appointments with instructors and counselors, and nonschool activities, such as appointments with the doctor, grocery shopping, picking up tickets, renewing licenses, etc. It is these nonstudy activities that tend to eat up study time. When you are learning how to plan, they must be considered or they will continue to keep you from studying.

Step 3: How Much Time Will It Take?
You probably have a good idea of this from the exercise in which you followed yourself around and recorded all your activities. Next to each item on your list, put down the time it will take to accomplish that assignment or task. In some cases you will have an accurate time idea, and in others you will have to estimate the time of completion. If you are estimating time, always give yourself more time than you believe it will take. It is always easier to eliminate time than to add time to an already busy schedule. If you did not complete the first step, you will have to use this estimation process.

Step 4: When (and Where) Will You Do It?
Since it is a good idea to consistently work (or study) in the same place, it follows that it is a good idea to work on specific subjects at a consistent time each day. This is a good way to develop mental discipline and improve concentration. The next step is to designate specific times for accomplishing homework and other tasks. Before you do this, look at the Fixed Commitments Schedule and note when you have free time. Now look at your "to do" list and fit the tasks to the times available. Remember some of the suggestions from Chapter 1. It is a good idea to study close to class time, study difficult subjects when you are feeling at your peak, vary your study activities, and break up study times into consecutive segments to match the time available.

How much time you allot to a task involves setting priorities—determining how much attention and effort a particular task deserves. A course that is a prerequisite to or part of your major subject may require a

TO DO LIST: Week of _____ 198_

TO DO	TIME ESTIMATES
Accounting Read Ch. 4, 20 pages, and work 3 problems. Due: 5 days	6 hours: 2 hours of reading, 3 to work problems, and 1 hour to review
Study Skills Read Ch. 7 & 8, 40 pages, edit one set lecture notes. Underline chapter to hand in. Due: 3 days.	3 hours; $1\frac{1}{2}$ hours to read, $\frac{1}{2}$ hour to edit, and 1 hour to underline
English Read Ch. on parts of speech (10 pages), make note-cards. Do exercise end of chapter. Test on parts. Due: 1 week	5 hours: 1 hour to read, 1 hour to make cards, 1 hour to do exercise, and 2 hours for review.
See Cslr. about major choice.	$\frac{1}{2}$ hour
Shop for birthday present for PM party	1 hour
Get tickets for Saturday game	15 minutes
Take Joe to work Thursday afternoon	$\frac{1}{2}$ hour

TO DO LIST: Week of _____ 198_

TO DO	TIME ESTIMATES	WHEN AND WHERE TO DO
Accounting Read Ch. 4, 20 pages, and work 3 problems. Due: 5 days	6 hours: 2 hours of reading, 3 to work problems, and 1 hour to review	Mon.-Tues. 9 A.M. at school. Tues. after dinner at home. Wed. before work at school and Thurs. P.M. at home.
Study Skills Read Ch. 7 & 8, 40 pages, edit one set lecture notes. Underline chapter to hand in. Due: 3 days.	3 hours; $1\frac{1}{2}$ hours to read, $\frac{1}{2}$ hour to edit, and 1 hour to underline	Tues. & Wed. 8 A.M., at school Wed. night (9 to 10:30 P.M. after work)
English Read Ch. on parts of speech (10 pages), make note-cards. Do exercise end of chapter. Test on parts. Due: 1 week	5 hours: 1 hour to read, 1 hour to make cards, 1 hour to do exercise, and 2 hours for review.	Monday, 3 P.M., before work. Monday, P.M., after work. Thurs. P.M. while waiting for Joe to finish class. In $\frac{1}{2}$-hour blocks on Friday (before party), Saturday (after work) & Sunday (before & after company).
See Cslr. about major choice.	$\frac{1}{2}$ hour	Friday during free hour
Shop for birthday present for PM party	1 hour	Friday 2 P.M.. on way home
Get tickets for Saturday game	15 minutes	On way to shopping center, Friday
Take Joe to work Thursday afternoon	$\frac{1}{2}$ hour	About 3:15 P.M.

lot of time. A course that is easy for you or is an elective may require less time. During a week when you have several exams, tasks such as reading for fun or working on a craft project may have to be given a lower priority. Even among the several tests, one may require more attention and study time than the others.

Time-planning by priority means keeping goals in mind. If completing your education is your number one goal, your time schedule will probably reflect it, with the greatest amount of time going into studying. As you review your schedule each week, note where you are spending the bulk of your time. Does your time expenditure reflect your priorities? Is it leading to the accomplishments of your goals, or are you spending more time at tasks that are not getting you where you want to go? Obviously, the first step is to learn what is important for you. It may be school, your job, or spending more time with your family or by yourself. The next thing is to make sure your schedule reflects these priorities, assigning more time to the most important priorities and less time to the least important. Go back and review the Time Analysis Form on pages 43–44 for help in setting your priorities.

Many students like to use a reward system for accomplishing scheduled tasks. All this means is taking time to do a favorite thing or activity as a reward for accomplishing a scheduled task.

A reward can be watching a favorite TV show, working on a hobby or project (craft or mechanical, etc.) for a fixed period of time (say one hour), or talking on the phone to a friend *after* completing an assigned task from your "to do" list.

You can even use assignments as rewards, doing the more favored subject after you complete an assignment in a less favored subject.

No one can make you feel better about you than yourself. Rewards give you something to look forward to, especially when a completed, less favored task is followed by a more favored one. Looking forward to spending time in a way you like, or with people you like, is a strong motivating force for accomplishing tasks that are less enjoyable.

List the activities you would want to use in setting up a reward system for work accomplished.

_____

_____

The idea of planning time so rigidly may cause some of you to have second thoughts about scheduling; you may wonder or even doubt whether you can live with so much structure. These are legitimate thoughts. No one ever said discipline is easy, especially if you have never scheduled your time before. Most students, however, find the rewards pleasant. For those not in the habit of time-planning, this method gives the necessary structure to begin forming new habits, but it also allows for weekly variation to suit your list, which will change from week to week. Once scheduling is a habit and you know yourself and your priorities better, you can become less fixed in your routine, trading off study time against other activities. Some students say they share their schedules, either by telling their plans to a family member, roommate, or friend, or by posting a schedule visible to all members of the household. The rewards for planning and consistent study behavior are a source of satisfaction. There is less anxiety and more time for yourself when work is well spaced.

SUMMARY

To improve your time use:
—Gather as much information about yourself, your habits, and the things you must do as possible.
—Become a list-maker. Write down what you have to do, how long it will take, and when you plan to do it.
—Set goals for getting things done. It eliminates a lot of wheel-spinning. Working by priority is usually more fruitful than running around to put out the brush fires as they spring up. It creates a positive tension. Things put off also create tension, but the stress associated with them is negative.
—Grade your tasks as to importance. Do it right away if it is both important and urgent. Do it soon if it is important but not urgent. Do it after you have completed tasks in the first two categories if it is neither important nor urgent. Things in the last category are usually the requests made by others for a piece of our time.
—Learn to say no. It is neither rude nor impolite but merely a preservation technique that assists you in carrying out your schedule.
—Learn to reward yourself for completing a job on time.

THE
EFFICIENT LEARNER:
GENERAL STUDY
SKILLS TECHNIQUES

II

LISTENING AND NOTE-TAKING | 4

This chapter is concerned with listening to lectures and note-taking techniques. It begins with a discussion of the listener's responsibilities during a lecture. It next suggests what to listen for and how to take notes during the lecture. Finally, it deals with what to do with your notes once the lecture is over.

Mentally review your abilities as a listener and as a note-taker. Complete the following statements:

When I listen, I _____

_____

_____

_____

When I take notes, I _____

_____

_____

_____

It seems that most of my problems in a lecture class are _____

_____

_____

_____

Therefore, based on the chapter content and your needs, the information you will want to pay particular attention to is _____

_____

_____

_____

LISTENING AS A SKILL

Listening, as well as note-taking, is a skill—as are most study techniques, for that matter. Skills are acquired, not natural, abilities. Students must therefore learn techniques and practice them till they are comfortable habits. Research suggests that people spend about half the day listening to others, and so it's important for you to analyze your skill as a listener and then work to improve those components in which you are weak.

Think about listening and the qualities that make a good listener. When you speak with someone, what makes you feel your messages have been heard? That you and the other party have communicated? You probably would say that you both looked at each other, you both heard the other's message, and each party responded to the message of the other. You both cleared up any misunderstandings in the conversation as they occurred, asking for clarification of ideas. Neither person prejudged or misjudged the other or put the other down by name-calling or labeling the other's ideas as stupid or irrelevant.

We can all give vivid examples of poor communication. Parties where there are a lot of people we either have not met before or don't care about usually provide examples of poor communication. Almost everyone has been guilty of speaking to a person while looking around the room for another person judged to be more interesting with whom he or she would rather talk. While one of you is looking around, the other is talking about the latest fad in food. The half attention you give the conversation causes the speaker's message to come across garbled. The speaker in turn responds with a statement that either is not on the subject or touches only a portion of the message which was heard. The response could be to fads in general or to food, but not to the latest fads in food. A frustrating experience for both parties, listener and speaker.

PREPARATION FOR LISTENING

As a student, you have heavy demands made on your skill as a listener. Every day you hear several lectures, with variations in style, purpose, and delivery by the instructors. In part, these variations reflect the speakers, in part the nature of the content about which they are speaking. Think for a minute! What makes a lecture interesting to you?

Perhaps your list includes such items as:

1. An interesting speaker
2. A lively person
3. Someone who uses visual aids, demonstrations, or anecdotal material
4. An interesting topic

It is true that some speakers are more interesting than others and are perhaps easier to listen to. Where is the listener's responsibility in all this? As a listener, you too have obligations: to be prepared, attentive, and actively engaged in the listening process.

THE LISTENER'S RESPONSIBILITIES

In order to get the most out of lecture classes, you must be prepared. This means knowing what you are going to hear. At the very least, it means being aware of the general topic to be discussed. This information can come directly from the lecturer's announcement of the subject of a particular lecture or more usually from following the syllabus carefully, and/or reading the assigned material before you go to the lecture. Not being prepared for a lecture is somewhat like taking a trip across the country without reading a road map. You have no idea where the mountains or rivers are or whether there are detours along the way. In other words, How do you get where you are going?

For example, a student taking a sociology course reads the syllabus and learns that both the lecture topic and the reading assignment are about family relationships. By reading the chapter beforehand, the student learns that there are three major types of kinship systems, notes the new vocabulary words related to the topic, and reads examples of family structures from both western and nonwestern cultures. Several of the vocabulary terms are new, and a few are not clear. This means that the student has a few questions which the lecture should help clear up. If not, the student knows that the instructor must be asked directly for clarification of the points in question.

After reading the assignment, the student thinks about the knowledge he or she already has about family relationships. Being a member of a family system, the student can think about the complexity of relationships. From a prior course, perhaps anthropology, the student recalls information on kinship and tries to relate it to the new information. A little preparation goes a long way toward tuning in to a lecture.

Now it's your turn. Think of all your courses in which you will attend a lecture soon—either later today or tomorrow. Answer the following questions in preparation for a lecture you are going to hear.

1. If there is a course syllabus, what topic is listed for discussion?

_____

2. Is there a text or other reading recommended?

_____

3. Have you read it?

_____

4. If you haven't, why not?

_____

5. If you have, what did you learn?

_____

6. What did you already know about the topic?

_____

7. How does what you read relate to what you will hear?

_____

8. What questions do you have from the reading that you want the lecture to clear up for you?

_____

If the lecturer uses the text as a basis for the lecture, you should never go to class without having read the assignment. Reading beforehand provides the information you need to follow the lecture. You can assess what you understand from the reading and list the topics you did not understand. Once the lecture has begun, you can mentally assess what you hear—reacting positively to those things you hear and know and listening carefully for those things you have questioned. You either will understand it from the lecture or will be able to raise a question when it is discussed; or you may decide to see the instructor after class. In any case, points not understood can be clarified immediately. Not doing this results in incomplete or unclear notes. This makes studying for and passing a test very difficult.

If the lecturer does not use the text as a basis for the lecture, reading beforehand in this case will provide you with a general map so that you can follow the lecturer and see where he or she is going with the information. For example, in business accounting, you may be asked to read the text to learn the theoretical ideas behind financial statements. The instructor assumes you know the background information and uses the class time to present and work through strictly practical problems related to the setting up of a company's financial statement.

In sociology, anthropology, or business law, you may read about concepts or ideas, and in class the instructor will illustrate the ideas by applying them to descriptions of societies or case studies. Without the background knowledge, what you hear and the notes you take will probably lack purpose and coherence.

Each lecture has a purpose: to recite the information from the text, to expand on it and provide information from the instructor's extensive background, or to make a practical application of the text material to particular situations.

WHAT'S IMPORTANT? HOW TO LOCATE IT

Listening involves two people: a speaker who presents material and a listener who must understand it. You could say it is like any game involving two people or partners. One helps the other, with each having a responsibility in the relationship. As the listener, or catcher if you think of it as a game of Frisbee, you must be aware of what the thrower is doing to send you the material and how you must be prepared to catch or rescue the oncoming missiles, in this case the words.

The lecturer uses a variety of delivery techniques. These include main ideas as well as details, illustrations, and case studies to support those ideas. A lecturer in psychology may begin by saying that neuroses are common but complex mental disorders (a main idea), go on to catalog the types of neuroses (supporting details), and then discuss some typical neurotic behaviors (case studies). The progress of the lecture is from the general to the specific.

On the other hand, a lecturer may start out with case studies, give each illustration a particular label, and sum it all up by saying that neuroses are common but complex mental disorders. The progress of this type of lecture is from the specific to the general.

Being aware of the structure the lecturer is using allows you to follow what is being said and to recognize the important points for note-taking.

In some courses, such as history; music, art, or literature surveys; or courses that present scientific theories or principles, the material can be presented chronologically. The lecturer proceeds in a time order, starting with the facts or ideas associated with the earliest date in the period being discussed and proceeding through to the end of the era.

In a science course, you will probably hear the lecturer presenting some material in a classifying pattern—a subject followed by a listing of subcategories. For example, a lecturer may start the course by saying that science is divided into two categories, natural and physical, and then go on to tell you the subcategories of each—the natural sciences being chemistry, physics, and math; and the physical sciences being biology, botany, physiology, and zoology.

In the sciences you will also hear processes analyzed. For example, the lecturer will give a step-by-step description of how the heart works or of the processes of mitosis or photosynthesis.

At some point, almost all lecturers will use contrasts and cause and effect patterns to explain material. When a lecturer contrasts two or more factors or ideas, he or she is showing the differences between them, for example, the writing style of two or more authors, the manner in which psychologists have looked at the concept of learning over the years, or the differences between accounting systems.

In order to show cause and effect, a lecturer will demonstrate the relationship between two things, such as a historical event and the reasons for its occurrence. For example, the lecturer may present the causes of the War of 1812—the economic, social, and political factors and their relationship to the war and its outcome.

Not all lecturers, however, are well-organized. It is harder to listen, to follow, and to take notes from a speaker who jumps around verbally. Always be prepared before you go to class.

Lecture presentations always include clue words, which are verbal hints as to what is important. Don't ignore these signals. A lecturer may introduce an idea by saying:

"There are several reasons why . . ."

"A major development in the cause of . . ."

"The most important . . ."

or signal supporting data for the main idea by saying:

"As an example . . ."

"For instance . . ."

"This leads us to see that . . ."

or further the discussion by saying:

"On the one hand . . ."

followed by

"On the other hand . . ."

"Furthermore . . ."

"Similarly . . ."

"In contrast . . ."

or conclude or summarize the discussion by saying:

"Therefore . . ."

"In conclusion . . ."

"Finally . . ."

"In summary . . ."

"Therefore, you will see . . ."

In addition, it is not uncommon for a lecturer to come right out and say, "This is important, write it down." Important ideas are frequently repeated.

Besides using your ears for the verbal clues, you must use your eyes for the visual clues as to what is important. These include items written on the blackboard or flashed from overhead projectors as well as slides and filmstrips.

Watch your lecturers carefully. Frequently, they read important material directly from their notes or a book to make sure *they* get it right and *you* get it down in your notes.

An instructor's physical actions are sometimes a signal for the importance of an idea. For example, a person who is a pacer may stand still when delivering an important idea. A eyeglass-wearer may remove them and look straight at the class. A desk-sitter may stand up. An off-the-cuff speaker may read from a paper or book.

As you can see, the nature of the course and its content frequently lend themselves to certain patterns of presentation by the lecturer. Many lecturers are well-organized, and it is easy to follow them and their lecture styles. Many are not. It makes good sense to be prepared for what you will hear and to be tuned in to the manner of presentation.

MENTAL ATTITUDES FOR LISTENING

Preparation for catching a lecture includes a good mental attitude. Tuning out can be easy if you let yourself get caught up in daydreaming, mental self-putdown, or trying to memorize while listening.

We all daydream. Actually, it is a fine way to turn over problems in one's mind or speculate on the future. However, daydreaming during a lecture (or during study sessions) is costly. The immediate implication is that you miss what is being said and therefore fail to get any notes.

What causes daydreaming in a classroom? For one thing, not being prepared. Inadequate preparation can make a lecture sound like just so much noise, and so your mind begins to wander. For another thing, the lecturer's pace may cause problems. Since your mind functions more quickly than the average person can speak (a person can chatter at only about 125 to 150 words a minute, while you can process ideas twice as fast), you and your mind race along, leaving the lecturer far behind.

You can also daydream, or at least set your mind off in another direction, if the lecturer says something with which you tend to disagree. Refusing to listen will not make you more correct than the speaker. Besides, it is the lecturer's opinion that probably will be called for on the test, whether you agree with it or not.

Lectures are no place to put yourself down. It is true that some lectures are more difficult than others, but it will be impossible to pay attention, and at the very least be able to put your finger on what you *don't* understand, if you are talking to yourself. If you catch yourself saying "I can't do this" or "I hate this subject and I'm just not able to learn it," you probably won't be able to learn it. A self-defeating attitude becomes a self-fulfilling prophecy.

Lectures are no place to try to memorize what the speaker is saying. It is not possible for you to know everything the speaker has said at the end of a fifty-minute lecture. Instead, go to the lecture prepared for what you will hear. Listen with an open mind so that you get the pattern, content, and sense of what is being said. Ask questions when you don't understand. Take the best set of notes you possibly can and study them right after the lecture.

NOTE-TAKING

Based on what has just been said about listening, it's clear that the first step in taking good lecture notes is thorough preparation before going to class. That implies reading or at least skimming the material to be discussed. Besides preparing you for the lecture, it gives you a chance to integrate what was just read with the course material presented earlier.

The next step is to get the notes down on paper during the lecture.

As with all the skills discussed in this book, note-taking is an active process meant to promote learning. The best preparation will go for nothing if you just sit and listen to the speaker without physically taking notes. Without notes, studying for exams based on lectures is impossible. Forgetting is hastened, and you lose concentration during the lecture. If you take notes, you will have a chance to sort out what you understand from what you yet need to understand. Presumably, the lecture will clear up the weak spots. If not, it should give you direct questions for clarification by the instructor.

Notes should be taken in pen on ruled, 8½ by 11 inch paper. Keep notes for each class together, either in a separate notebook or in separate sections of the same notebook.

Draw a line down about one-third of the way across the page. This creates a superwide margin to be used for study purposes after the lecture. Your paper will look like this:

```
┌──────┬──────────────────────────────────────────┐
│      │        Topic:_____   Date:_____    │
│   •  │                                           │
│      │                                           │
│      │                                           │
│   •  │                                           │
│      │                                           │
│      │                                           │
│   •  │                                           │
│      │                                           │
└──────┴──────────────────────────────────────────┘
```

Whenever possible, notes should be in your own words, in brief phraselike form. Obviously, things written on the board or given in the form of other visual clues, as well as direct verbal clues from the instructor, should be written as they appear or as the instructor speaks them. However, you do have time to put most things in your own words. Doing so reinforces the fact that you understood what was said.

Try to leave a lot of blank space in your notes. Look at the two sets of notes below. From which one would you rather study?

Example 4.1 is what I call wall-to-wall notes. They are busy, crowded, and most of all, hard to read for study purposes. Example 4.2 represents clear, uncrowded, easy-to-read notes.

Note-taking is another reinforcement mechanism in the learning process. When you read the material, you see it. When you listen to a lecture on the same material, you hear it. When you write the material

EXAMPLE

4.1
Wall-to-wall notes

— Studying a foreign language very different from other courses
  — Don't cram
  — Cumulative effort means studying every day
  — Time spent studying more necessary than motivation
— Ways language is taught
  — Focus on vocabulary — must study sentence construction, verb conjugations, and vocabulary
  — Focus on conversation — must study by going over conversations, not grammar.
  — Pronunciation is important — must speak language a lot with others to hear sounds (even pronounce in class to yourself while others speak)
  — Translation — 2 possible techniques — Guess from context — used in conversation-focused course — does not depend on dictionary meanings that are precise and accurate — combination of both methods probably best.
  — Other Study Aids — Writing translations in the book — bad idea — don't learn to think in the language and become dependent on your notes — also poor for review purposes.
  Vocabulary Flash cards — very helpful — can carry around for small, quick study sessions; can shuffle for not learning in a rote way, can space practice
  — Language Exams — Will reflect the teaching style used in class — slow, accurate translation emphasizing grammar and vocabulary — or approximate translations. Use good exam prep techniques — predicting questions in advance — recite a lot.

down, you feel it. The physical action of writing involves coordination of your eyes, your ears, and the motor action of your hand. Reinforcing the same material through the different sense modalities is an aid to learning.

When you read, you see print. It is possible to go back to the print and reread. A lecturer's words are lost as they are spoken. In order to have a record of what was said so that you will not forget the lecture material, you must take notes. Even if you understand everything the lecturer is saying, write it down anyway.

EXAMPLE

4.2
Well-spaced notes

<u>STUDYING A FOREIGN LANGUAGE</u>

Different Kinds of study required

- No cramming possible
- Cumulative effort means study every day
- Time spent studying more necessary than motivation

Ways Language is Taught

Focus on the vocabulary	Focus on conversation
① must study sentence construction	① must study by going over conversations, not grammar
② verb conjugations	
③ vocabulary	

Pronunciation is important
- must speak language a lot with others to hear sounds (Even pronounce in class to yourself while others speak.)

Translation — 2 Possible Techniques
- Guess from context
  - used in conversation- focused course
  - Does not depend on dictionary definition but what sense you make of word meaning from words around it.
- Use dictionary
  - used in vocabulary - focused course
  - Depends on dictionary meanings that are precise and accurate.
  - Combination of both methods is probably best

- Other Study Aids
  - Writing translation in the book
    - Bad idea— don't learn to think in the language and become dependent on your notes
    - Also poor for review purposes

EXAMPLE

4.2
Continued.

— Vocabulary flash cards
— very helpful — can carry around for small, quick study sessions
— can shuffle for not learning in rote way
— can space practice

Language Exams
— Will reflect the teaching style used in class — slow, accurate approximate translations
— Use good exam prep techniques — predicting questions in advance
— Recite a lot

Some Further Note-taking Techniques

Good notes are taken in a modified outline format. While not following the formal structure of an outline, they do make use of many of the principles, such as indenting, headings to label ideas, and markers to identify points under each heading. These markers can be in the form of numbers, letters, dashes, or asterisks (*). Select a system that is comfortable for you, and stick to it.

Many students prefer to write on one side of the page. By leaving the back side blank, they create space for book notes, for examples and drawings (this is especially good in math and science classes), and for indexing the notes to reflect only the essentials needed for study purposes.

If you take notes on only one side of the page, as recommended for math and science, the back side of the previous page becomes your editing space. Formulas, sample problems, or scientific processes or diagrams can be simplified and made usable for exam preparation. In Example 4.3, two problems were taken down. The edited notes on the facing page are explanations of the two types of probability, namely, the formulas and the verbal equivalents of the symbols.

If the lecturer is well-organized or puts an outline of the talk on the board, note-taking is usually made considerably easier than if the lecturer is disorganized or repetitious.

The key to note-taking in a rapid lecture is preparation and a quick hand. Your job will be to get as much down as quickly as possible. You might try raising your hand to ask a question, thereby slowing the speech down. If that's not possible, try the buddy system. You and several others slip carbon paper between the sheets of your notebooks. After the lecture, share your notes, thereby picking up missed points and a complete set of notes from the work of others.

If the lecturer is disorganized and jumps around a lot, you will have to follow as best you can. Leave a lot of blank space; when you hear a point being made that belongs several topics back, just backtrack and try to fit it in where it belongs. This won't be possible if you take wall-to-wall notes, however.

Should you use a tape recorder at a lecture? Generally not. What it really means is that you are listening to the same lecture twice, once in class and once at home. Most students do not have that much time. Learn to listen and take notes the first time—during the lecture. Don't depend on a machine. However, if you are doing extremely poorly in a course, or if the lecturer is very disorganized, or if you have a language or writing problem, it is a good idea to use a tape recorder. In the first two cases, use the machine only till you get the hang of the course or the lecturer's style. Don't become dependent on it. In the latter case, you may have to use a machine for an extended time. Whatever your situation, check with the instructor before doing the actual recording. Many people do not like to be recorded, especially without their knowledge. Also check with the learning resource center. Many provide this service for students with learning or language handicaps.

ONCE THE LECTURE IS OVER

The most important part of the process begins when the lecture is over— going over the notes taken during the lecture, editing them, and making them useful for study purposes.

Notes taken and not edited for studying soon become "cold" and useless. Notes hampered by errors in content, omission of important data, or poor organization, or even good notes left unread and un-organized, are usually impossible to reread and comprehend two or three weeks after they are taken. That's just about when you need them for test purposes.

Each day after class (preferably after each lecture but for sure at the end of the day), read the notes you took that day in each class. The purpose is to edit your notes. Editing is not necessarily a recopying process. Just rewriting the originals more neatly is not a learning process but a mechanical act. The purpose of editing is to increase understanding of the material by organizing it for future use. This means making additions or corrections, labeling and numbering points, and indexing or outlining notes. Here's the place where a large empty margin comes into use.

EXAMPLE

4.3
Explanation of statistics notes on previous page

PROBABILITY— means finding area under normal curve or proportion or percentage of cases that something is going to happen

2 Types

(A) Have to get

Probability

Formula =
$$z = \frac{x - M}{O}$$

z = probabilty
x = score
M = mean
O = stand. dev.

(B) given Probability—Have to get scores or critical areas that correspond to that probability

Formula =
$$x = O(z) + M$$

x = score
O = stand. dev.
z = z score from table
M = mean

A well-taken set of notes may only have to be gone over for indexing—using the margin for extracting and outlining the main ideas and subpoints or pinpointing the important terminology or data. See Example 4.4.

This example of a well-taken set of notes comes from an anthropology lecture on "Witchcraft" given by Naomi Goldenberg. It shows that the only task to be done after the lecture is to go through and index the notes for ease in studying. With the main points highlighted in the margin, you need only cover the notes and use the highlights as a memory trigger for easy reciting and reviewing.

Notice the use of the symbol = instead of writing out the word "equals" each time it is used. Also note the insertion of information to help explain some of the points in the notes: "crops, birth, and death" to explain cyclical events, and "older woman" to explain the word "crone." These insertions can be made during the lecture or when you edit.

The content of each course lends itself to a set of symbols or abbreviations for use in lecture notes. Certain words or symbols appear

EXAMPLE

4.3
Notes taken from a statistics lecture

STATISTICS   Date
PROBABILITY

① given a score x
② standardize score
③ Enter normal table & find probability

Type Ⓐ Problem - given a normal
pop. w̄ M = 100 and O = 15, find the
probability that something is going
to happen falling below a score of 108

$$\frac{108-100}{15} = 8/15 = .53$$

z = 0.53 ——— Fz = .7019
Probability is 70 if we drew a sample
that it would be below 108

① given a probability, what score corresponds to it
② Enter table
③ Read z score
④ Translate it to either x or x̄

Type Ⓑ Problem - what score in a
normal population corresponds to
the value which has 10% of the
cases above it —
The mean = 50 and SO = 5

$$1.28(5) + 50$$
$$6.40 + 50 = 56.4$$
$$Score = 56.4$$

repeatedly. This means that consistency is important if you use abbreviations or symbols.

If you are taking psychology, for example, you can use a capital P or the symbol for psychology, Ψ, to abbreviate the word each time it appears in your notes. Courses in such areas as math, science, and engineering abound in potential abbreviations and symbols. Use them wisely.

Notes with too many abbreviations are hard to reread. So are notes with too few or inconsistently used abbreviations. Where abbreviations and symbols already exist, learn and use them wisely. Where they do not, create your own and use them consistently.

Still another way to edit a well-taken set of notes is to highlight the main topics and then turn any appropriate headings into questions. It

EXAMPLE

4.4
Well-taken set of notes indexed to reveal the main points

Anthropology 101   Date _____

Lecture on "Witchcraft"

Witchcraft *- pagan (def.)* *- 2 concerns* *① cyclical* *events* *② healing*	*Witchcraft is a pagan religion* *— word "pagan" means "of the earth"* *— deals with cyclical events (crops,* *birth, death) and basic healing*
Organization *Coven (13)* *Grove (50)*	*Witches Organization* *— Local unit = coven - 13 people* *to a coven (12 + 1 leader) (12* *handmaidens + 1 priestess)* *— Grove - 50 or more witches*
Moon as Symbol *Phases = types*	*Main Symbol = Moon* *Phases of moon = witch types* *Emerging crescent = virgin* *Full moon = Queen* *Waning moon = Crone (older woman)*
2 Traditions *① Dianic* *② Gardnerian*	*Varied Traditions in Witchcraft* *Dianic - After godess Diana* *only woman in this coven* *Gardnerian - from Gerald* *Gardner both men & women* *many hetero covens* *appear to have homo-* *sexual orientation*

makes the main ideas easy to read and review. Just cover the page; as each topic is revealed, answer the question by reciting the material aloud. Then check yourself for accuracy. See Example 4.5.

Notes that lack important information need to have additions made to the content. Suppose the lecturer said that there were four reasons "why" and you only had time to get three points down, or you may be missing a math problem or case study. To fill in the missing material, turn to the text, look at another student's notes, or ask the instructor to help fill in the missing material.

EXAMPLE

4.5

Anthropology 101   Date____

Witchcraft

What is meant by
| witchcraft is a "pagan religion"? |

- word "pagan" means "of the earth"
- deals with cyclical events (crops, birth, death)
  and basic healing

what is
| Witches Organization? |

- Local unit = coven - 13 people to a coven
  (12 + 1 leader) 12 handmaidens + 1 priestess
- grove = 50 or more witches

what is
| main Symbol of witchcraft and what does it mean? |

- main symbol = moon
- Phases of moon = witch types
     - Emerging Crescent = virgin
     - Full moon   = Queen
     - Waning moon   = Crone (older woman)

name the
| Varied Traditions in Witchcraft? |

- Dianic - After godess Diana
              (only women in coven)
- Gardnerian - from Gerald Gardner
              both men and women
              many hetero covens
              tend to have homosexual orientation

Let's continue with the set of notes on "Witchcraft." Suppose that in the segment on the tools used by witches, the instructors went so rapidly that you failed to get all the information down. The first set of sample notes (Example 4.6) represents what a student was able to get down on paper during the lecture. Example 4.7 demonstrates the addition of missed information during the editing process. When an item was missed, a space was left for it. The names of the four elements were inserted as well as an explanation of a "natural" material in the case of the altar.

By numbering the items in your notes during the editing process, you make them a little clearer to read. Also note that the student added a topic title so that the notes were labeled as to content.

Some Further Editing Techniques

Even adequate notes may lack identifying tags that make them easier to read. One topic may follow another without a break; or if the topics are labeled, the points underneath may not be. The editing process is when you should label and identify topics as well as the supporting details.

There are several systems you can use. In some of the examples given here, dashes (--) are used to represent a new idea and distinguish

EXAMPLE

4.6
Notes with information missing

Anthropology 101   Date ____

Altar — natural Materials

Altar cloth — + pictures of gods, godesses
                              + mirror

Four Elements — Symbols
Dagger
Wands
Cup @ water — to see future visions

Ren —— 5 pointed star

Cord — 9 ft. long

Rugs, necklaces, items with circles
          amulets, talismans.

EXAMPLE

4.7
Missing information inserted during editing process

Anthropology 101   Date___

Tools Witches use to Conduct Rituals

① Altar – Natural Materials (Stone or Wood)

② Altar cloth – + pictures of gods, god-
   desses & mirror

③ Four Elements – Symbols for earth,
   air, fire, water

④ Dagger — with magnatized blade
   (to call, attract spirits)

⑤ Wands – cut from 1 of 13 trees, used
   to focus the will

⑥ Cup @ water – to see future visions

⑦ Pentacle — 5 pointed star
   star painted up – also made
   of natural material

⑧ Cord 9 ft. long — worn around waist

⑨ Cauldron——place for stirring up
   something

⑩ Rings, necklaces, items @ circles,
   amulets, tailsmans

one level of idea from another. In others, letters or numbers are used to identify each idea. Whether you use a system of dashes or a system of numbers or letters, be consistent and stick to the same symbols throughout. Underlining makes an item stand out for easy rereading. Also note the large amount of empty space left in the sample notes. This allows for the insertion of material when you are taking the notes or later in the editing process.

It is sometimes necessary to take summary notes (Example 4.8). This is especially true in recitation classes or courses in which ideas rather than facts are discussed, such as literature, philosophy, or sociology. In recitation classes, the discussion is led by the instructor on material already covered in class. The purpose is to give the student a chance to

EXAMPLE

4.8
Summary notes with editing

Marketing Seminar   Date ____
Topic – ADVERTISING

But does it in raise price in any instances?

In general advertising reduces price of goods for consumer – with more goods produced, they can lower the price.

Possible test question – give an example or write an advertisement for each of these categories

Distinction made between primary advertising which promotes an entire class of goods vs brand advertising which promotes a name brand

Different kinds – newspapers, magazines, radio, T.V., direct mail, outdoor advertising, bus & car cards, free samples

Went over many forms of advertising – looking at samples from different media.

talk through some of the ideas already mentioned by the lecturer and read in the text. Since the material is fairly well known and you probably have lecture notes on the body of the content, and since there are many people speaking rather than just one lecturer, it is best to summarize the points being made every once in a while rather than take notes constantly throughout the discussion. Summary notes can be edited by putting the main idea in the margin or by making a notation comparing or relating the discussion topic to the lecture or anticipating possible test questions.

RECITING AND REVIEWING

Regardless of whether you take notes in outlines that use whole sentences or phrases or make summary or paragraph notes, the best set of notes will be forgotten if not gone over immediately after editing and frequently thereafter.

Once your notes are edited, spend a few more minutes reciting the key points—the highlighted topics, the important terminology, and the key material extracted from your notes. Remember, recitation ensures remembering.

Most students find it useful to review all their notes once each week. The obvious advantages are that it aids retention and cuts down on both anxiety and preparation time before an exam. Test preparation then becomes a matter of review, not relearning.

SUMMARY

Before the lecture:
    —Be prepared—know about what you are going to hear.
    —Be a good listener—use good listening skills.
    —Be prepared to take notes.
During the lecture:
    —Take notes according to the lecturer's style and the nature of the subject matter.
    —Use your own words to record the ideas as much as possible.
    —Leave a lot of blank space on the paper.
    —Use a modified outline format.
After the lecture:
    —Go over the notes as soon after the lecture as possible.
    —Edit your notes by adding to or subtracting from them, labeling major and minor points, and indexing or outlining.
    —Review and recite the material in your notes on a regular basis as advance preparation for test-taking.

TEXTBOOKS: READING AND RETAINING

This chapter is concerned with reading textbooks. It presents material on how texts are organized and the kinds of information presented in textbooks. It suggests ways to preview a text and its chapters before reading and describes a systematic approach to the reading process itself. The final section presents information and exercises on the various kinds of notes taken from text material for the purpose of retention and test-taking.

Mentally review your attitude toward and experiences with textbook reading. Complete the following statements.

When I read textbooks, I usually feel _____

_____

_____

_____

In the past, my experience with textbooks has been _____

_____

_____

_____

Therefore, based on your comments and what you believe you need to learn about textbooks, in order to get the most out of this chapter, you will want to pay particular attention to information in the following areas:

_____

_____

_____

_____

Text reading constitutes one of the largest sections of this book, because it represents one of the biggest chunks of your college work. Texts present many problems to students unused to large reading assignments.

What do you say to yourself when faced with a large text-reading assignment? Write down your thoughts. _____

_____

_____

_____

Here are some of the comments heard from students in a study skills class:

"The book is boring."
Textbooks generally don't read like novels. There is not much action, few interesting characters, and little plot. Textbooks are meant to provide students with the basic data they need to know in an introductory course or the more advanced knowledge required for a specialized major area or professionally oriented course. Whether a text is boring will depend on you. While it is acknowledged that some authors do not do as good a job at text writing as others, regardless of the quality of the text, you are going to have to read it to pass the course. "Boring" is a state of mind, not a fact of life. To alter your state of mind, you have to change your habits and attitudes. A boring day requires you to get involved by making plans to see people or do things. A boring book requires you to take an active interest in the subject matter by doing the reading on time, as well as questioning, note-taking, and reciting to keep up and maintain a standard of performance. You can't like everything, but you can do the best job possible.

"I can't remember everything I read."
Text reading does not imply text memorization. Your job is to understand what you read, not memorize it. It is not unlike a lecture in the sense that on first reading, as on first learning, understanding is all that's required. It is only after you select and write down the important ideas from a chapter that the memorization process begins.

"I don't understand the ideas in the book."
It is not unreasonable to have problems understanding the ideas in a text, especially in a subject area which you have never studied before and in which you lack background. An example of this might be an introductory

course in philosophy. The question is, How do you improve your understanding?

First of all, you might try building some background by going to a source book. If you are having difficulty understanding the writings and ideas of Plato, read a general encyclopedia article that will give background on his life, time, and basic ideas. To understand a person's work, it is usually necessary to understand where he or she is coming from. A simpler version of your text reading would also help clarify a complicated text. Students in science courses frequently go back to a younger brother's or sister's or their own children's high school text in chemistry or biology, read a section on the material with which they are in trouble, and then reread their own text. If you can understand it in simpler terms, you will probably be able to grasp the more difficult wording of your own book. This is also very true in math courses, where the resolution of an equation or a proof is difficult to grasp in the text but understandable in a simpler college text that goes into the same material.

Reading comprehension does not only mean what you "get" or understand as a result of reading. It means you have to give to the page to get something from it. If you bring little, you get little. If you bring much, by reading an outside source or understanding the concept in a simpler form from reading another book or article on the subject, your understanding is likely to be increased in the give and take of learning.

"I can't understand the vocabulary words in the book."
Vocabulary accounts for a large percentage of the material to be learned in any introductory course. Therefore, by "vocabulary" we mean the words directly connected with the content as well as the words which constitute the author's writing style.

Course-specific words have special meanings that often are quite different from the meanings you have always understood. For example, what's your definition for the word "solid"? You probably would say "strong" or "sturdy." However, in science it means something very specific, namely, a substance that doesn't flow or pour; and in geometry it is an element having three dimensions, such as a cube.

Your definition for "work" would probably be "to do a job." However, in science it means "to exert an influence or force over."

The first step in understanding the vocabulary of a course is to learn the meanings of any familiar (or unfamiliar) words in relation to their specific usage within the context of the course.

List any familiar words you know and their specialized meanings within the context of course-specific material.

FAMILIAR WORD	MEANING IN COURSE-SPECIFIC CONTEXT

Comprehension is difficult when an author uses long, unfamiliar vocabulary words as part of the writing style. A lot of time can be spent looking the words up in a dictionary. Sometimes a reader steps over the word entirely, making the sentence or paragraph incomprehensible. The first method is not efficient, and the second is not effective. You don't have time to look up every word in the dictionary, and you can't step over words because the rest of the material will fail to make sense. It is better to try to get the meaning of the word from the context—the words and ideas that surround it. It will not be a dictionary definition, but that's all right so long as your reading makes sense. Resort to the dictionary for those few words for which you can't divine a meaning. Once you get the meaning from context, you'll be able to recognize it when it's used again, and authors do tend to repeat themselves.

Look at the following sentence. "Formal transfer of stock certificate titles is normally handled by a fiduciary agent, usually a bank, that will issue a new certificate in the name of the new owner of the shares."

Based on the context, define the term "fiduciary" agent. _____

If you said a strong or sound financial institution, you're close enough. The fact that an example, a bank, is given helps make the definition clearer. In actuality, the dictionary definition states that "fiduciary" means "trusted."

"I have too much to read in the time I have available."
This comment usually results from poor time-planning. Most instructors give reasonable assignments, and lengthy assignments usually have longer time limits for completion. Many students persist in doing all their

reading for a subject at a single sitting instead of dividing it into convenient segments. This is both frustrating and an ineffective study technique rather than an efficient, effective method of text reading. If you have three days to read two chapters covering sixty pages, read twenty pages a day. Remember, material studied over several days is more effectively learned than material crammed in at one sitting.

In the same manner, collateral reading, or supplementary books, should be read over time. Most instructors assign this type of material long in advance. Slipping in a few pages of an extra assignment each day rather than devoting a few days to hastily reading an outside book will not put you behind in all your other subjects and will probably result in a better understanding of the outside book.

ORGANIZATIONAL ASPECTS OF TEXT MATERIAL

Reading Comprehension

Since reading is such a large part of academic work, it's a good idea to be aware of the way text reading material is organized. It is also a good idea to know something about your skill as a reader. In a learning skills lab, you can learn more about your individual ability and receive help in any area in which you need extra work.

Comprehension of the written word is highly dependent on what you bring to the printed page. In other words, the more widely you have read, the more experiences you have gained, and the more you will have available to draw on for comprehending written material. While it is true that you learn from the printed page, you also must bring something to it in order to get the full benefit of what it is saying. It is important to make associations between what you know and what you are reading. Unfortunately most college students don't fall in the category of wide readers—those people who read a lot, thereby gaining the necessary background with which to approach their college texts. Answer the following questions about your attitudes toward and skill in reading.

What are your experiences as a reader?

_____

How would you evaluate your skill as a reader?

_____

How frequently do you read material other than texts?

_____

What kinds of material do you enjoy reading?

_____

What is your favorite book?

_____

What do you say to yourself when you can't understand a passage you are reading?

_____

Information in Textbooks

Textbooks are written to communicate certain basic types of information to the student.

DEFINITION OF TERMS

Since vocabulary accounts for such a large part of most courses, writers of textbooks use a large amount of space to define terms that are specific to the course content. The definition is given either directly or in the form of an example from the course content.

COMPARISON AND CONTRAST

This type of writing is meant to tell you how two or more things are alike or different in two or more ways.

ORDER OF EVENTS

This type of writing lays out the sequence in which things occur. For example: the events leading to a historic battle, the hierarchies in the plant or animal kingdoms, the different periods of geologic development, or the sequence in which a nurse performs hospital chores.

CATEGORIES

This type of writing places large amounts of facts into distinctly separate areas or categories. For example: a discussion of the nature of diseases that are then categorized as viral versus bacterial or an explanation of the characteristics of soil erosion that are then categorized by method, i.e., wind, water, etc.

HOW TO DO THINGS

This type of writing is used for giving directions on how to perform a task. For example: illustrations of a math problem indicating the steps in the sequence for solving it or a science lab manual which lays out the steps for doing lab experiments in chemistry, biology, or physics.

WHY THINGS ARE THE WAY THEY ARE

This type of writing is heavily factual and attempts to explain, through the use of facts, why a concept or function operates the way it does. For example: an explanation of the development of humans using the theory of evolution as the reason for present-day men and women.

POINTS OF VIEW

This type of writing presents the opinions and/or beliefs of the writer. Techniques such as giving the pros and/or cons or the advantages and/or disadvantages are commonly used. For example: a political science text may point out the advantages versus disadvantages of the democratic system, or a science book may point out the pros and cons of nuclear power.

How Paragraphs Are Organized

Paragraphs are written with a central theme or main idea and the enlargement of that idea through the use of facts, details, or examples. The reader must recognize the main idea and then relate the details or examples to it in order to understand the theme of the paragraph.

Main ideas can appear in three places: at the beginning, in the middle, or at the end of a paragraph. In the following three examples, the important thing to note is that the general sense remains the same. In each case, the paragraph is concerned with the thought "Good résumés have six sections" and is backed up with the facts—what those sections are and what is contained in each one. (See Examples 5.1, 5.2, 5.3.)

Some paragraphs have no main idea. Each sentence is just as important as the next. Such paragraphs are usually descriptive in nature (Example 5.4). Each sentence in this paragraph fits into the one preceding it, and they all go together to describe the biological classification scheme.

EXAMPLE

5.1
Main idea at the beginning

A well-constructed résumé provides information to a prospective employer in six different categories. The *personal facts* section contains your name, address, telephone number, and social security number. This is usually followed by a sentence naming the *specific job objective* for which your résumé has been prepared. The *education* section gives the name, place, dates of attendance, and degrees or certificates awarded for all the institutions you attended back to high school. The *experience* section details the jobs you have had, paid or unpaid, and lists the skills and responsibilities associated with each one. An *interest and activities* statement lists your hobbies, personal interests and achievements, and community and extra-curricular activities. At the bottom is a statement suggesting that *references* will be sent on request or the names and addresses of at least three references.

Example

5.2
Main idea in the middle

    A résumé begins with a *personal facts* section that contains your name, address, telephone number, and social security number. This is usually followed by a *job objective* statement, a sentence naming the specific job objective for which your résumé has been prepared. The education section gives the name, place, dates of attendance, and degrees or certificates awarded for all the institutions you attended back to high school. These are but three of the categories contained in a résumé. A well-constructed résumé provides information to a prospective employer in six different categories. The *experience* section details the jobs you have had, paid or unpaid, and lists the skills and responsibilities associated with each one. An *interests and activities* statement lists your hobbies, personal interests and achievements, and community and extracurricular activities. At the bottom is a statement suggesting that *references* will be sent on request or the names and addresses of at least three references.

Example

5.3
Main idea at the end

    A résumé begins with a *personal facts* section which contains your name, address, telephone number, and social security number. This is usually followed by a *job objective* statement, a sentence naming the specific job objective for which your résumé has been prepared. The *education* section gives the name, place, dates of attendance, and degrees or certificates awarded for all the institutions you attended back to high school. The *experience* section details the jobs you have had, paid or unpaid, and lists the skills and responsibilities associated with each one. An *interests and activities* statement lists your hobbies, personal interests and achievements, and community and extracurricular activities. At the bottom is a statement suggesting that *references* will be sent on request or the names and addresses of at least three references. Therefore, you can see that a well-constructed résumé provides information to a prospective employer in six different categories.

Example

5.4
Descriptive paragraph

    The formal biological system of classification is also hierarchic. Every kind of organism, called a species, belongs to a genus. Each genus belongs to a family. Each family belongs to an order and each order to a class. Every class is in a phylum, and every phylum is in a kingdom.

SOME BACKGROUND IDEAS

Learning in general, and reading content material in particular, is an active process. As a student, you must get involved with the subject in order to learn and retain it. Before a study method for texts is presented, you should be aware of some basic background information that will help you understand why some of the steps in the process are necessary for reading and understanding textbooks.

Previewing Reading Material

Previewing reading material contributes to the efficiency of the reading process by providing a road map of the chapter terrain. Stimulating interest before reading through a chapter allows you to see the structure of the chapter, or how the author presents the material, including the main topics and supporting material as well as the study aids.

Knowing the nature of the content and how it is presented helps stimulate interest and promotes an increased reading rate.

Reinforcing the Reading Material

Forgetting takes place very rapidly, just about immediately after learning, unless it is reinforced by taking notes, reciting, and reviewing.

Writing, in the form of book notes, underlining in the text, or charting the information, reinforces learning by stimulating another sense modality, the kinesthetic.

Memory is enhanced through recitation and review. Material read and not recited is forgotten at a rapid rate—50 percent is remembered by the day after reading, and little more than 20 percent is retained after several weeks. That's about the interval at which most instructors schedule exams.

A TEXT STUDY SYSTEM

The Whole Book

Before reading any part of the book, it is necessary to get an idea of the whole book.

Previewing the book before the course begins will give you an idea of the course content and the difficulty of the material, as well as ideas on the layout of the text, which will suggest ideas and possible approaches to it as a tool in your work in the course for which the book is assigned or required. Reading a text by jumping into it without a preview can be likened to jumping into a body of water without knowing the temperature or depth, both of which could be crucial to survival once you are immersed.

Previewing a Text

Previewing your texts, or any books for that matter, means spending time investigating them before the first reading assignment. You will have to answer the questions which appear below to get a good overview of what the book is all about. Several preview exercises are included. Use one for this book and the rest for the texts in your other courses.

TEXT PREVIEW QUESTIONNAIRE

Title of book: _____

Author: _____

Publisher: _____

Year published: _____

Check to see how many major study aids are included in the text:

Table of contents	_____	Glossaries: End of book _____
		End of chapters _____
Index	_____	Exercises, questions, or problems _____
Suggestions for further reading	_____	Pictures _____
Chapter previews	_____	Maps _____
Chapter summaries	_____	Graphs and charts _____

Look at the table of contents:

Into how many major sections is the book divided? _____

How many chapters are in the book? _____

How many chapters are in each section? _____

How are the chapters arranged? Chronologically? _____

Geographically? _____

Are there subheadings listed under each chapter's major heading?

Yes _____ No _____

If so, what ideas do you get about the scope or nature of each chapter?

Very broad? _____ Narrow and detailed? _____

Review the information you gathered from previewing the text. List the major concerns and ideas you gathered about the book. Consult your instructor or the learning skills specialist to assist you with anything you feel will be a major problem.

TEXT PREVIEW QUESTIONNAIRE

Title of book: _____

Author: _____

Publisher: _____

Year published: _____

Check to see how many major study aids are included in the text:

Table of contents	_____	Glossaries: End of book	_____
		End of chapters	_____
Index	_____	Exercises, questions, or	
		problems	_____
Suggestions for		Pictures	_____
further reading	_____		
Chapter previews	_____	Maps	_____
Chapter summaries	_____	Graphs and charts	_____

Look at the table of contents:

Into how many major sections is the book divided? _____

How many chapters are in the book? _____

How many chapters are in each section? _____

How are the chapters arranged? Chronologically? _____

Geographically? _____

Are there subheadings listed under each chapter's major heading?

Yes _____ No _____

If so, what ideas do you get about the scope or nature of each chapter?

Very broad? _____ Narrow and detailed? _____

THE PARTS OF THE BOOK: CHAPTERS

The system presented here for reading text chapters contains six basic steps. It incorporates ideas discussed earlier in this chapter that promote efficient learning. All the steps are necessary at some time in the learning process. Previewing and reading are done for understanding the material.

Note-taking, or any of the other systems mentioned in the next section of this chapter, is done for selecting the material to be remembered. Reciting and reviewing are done for retention of the material.

Step 1: Preview the Chapter

This is a brief process that should take less than five minutes of your time. The purpose is to note the general layout of the chapter, including the arrangement of the content (by topic, chronologically, etc.) as well as the study aids presented by the author (section headings and subheadings, illustrations, graphs, maps, charts, vocabulary words, summaries, and end-of-chapter questions or exercises). Your purpose for reading the chapter should be clear. It may be to learn a process (as in biology), follow a sequence of events (as in history) or an argument (as in psychology, philosophy, or political science), or learn how to solve or complete a problem (as in math or accounting).

Your purpose and judgment regarding the difficulty level of the reading will help you determine approximately how much time it will take you to read the chapter. A long chapter may have to be broken down into more than one study period to avoid fatigue, boredom, or both.

To preview a chapter:

- Look at the chapter title.

- Look at each major heading.

- Look at the subheadings within each section.

- Read a sentence or two in the opening paragraphs at the beginning of a section that is not clear to you.

- Note any visual aids: illustrations, charts, vocabulary in italics.

- Read the summary at the end of the chapter.

- Look at the end-of-chapter questions or exercises.

- State the chapter structure and the major ideas you got from skimming.

- Determine your purpose for reading the chapter.

- Weigh the difficulty level of the chapter in relation to your knowledge and reading skills.

- Estimate the time it will take you to read the chapter or portion of the chapter.

- Using either this book or another text, skim a chapter while following the guide questions and fill in the information you gather.

- Book title _____
- Chapter title _____
- Number of pages in chapter _____
- List the major chapter headings and some subheadings:

  Major heading _____

  Subheadings _____

  _____

  _____

  _____

  _____

  _____

  _____

  _____

- List the visual aids used in the chapter:

  _____

  _____

- State the major ideas of the chapter:

  _____

  _____

- State your purpose for reading the chapter: _____

  _____

- State the difficulty level of the chapter:

  Very   Somewhat   Not at all
  difficult _____ difficult _____ difficult _____

- How many pages are there in the chapter? _____
- Estimate the time it will take you to read the chapter: _____
- Would it be better to read it at one time or divide it into more than one

  study session? _____
  If you divide it, approximately how long would you estimate each

  reading session to be? _____

Step 2: Read the Chapter

Although this seems obvious, how you read a chapter of text material may vary with your purpose, the difficulty of the material, or your reading skills (all determined in the previewing step).

Most students find it best to read small sections of a chapter at a time—all the material under one heading or subheading. As a rule, a central idea is presented, backed up by data or related to material in a previous section, or an idea for the following section is set up. Reading too much at one time, say the entire chapter, makes steps 3 and 4 more difficult.

Step 3: Finding the Author's Ideas and Structure

After you've read a section of the chapter, you should mentally ask yourself two questions:

What did the author say that I have to learn?
How was it said?

The answer to the first question checks your understanding of the content; the answer to the second, your understanding of the structure, including whether the author used a major idea and details, a cause and effect argument, a case study, etc. This will help you determine what you must learn from your reading as well as the form your notes or underlining will take. It becomes a point of frustration if your answer seems confused or unclear, forcing you to go back over the material, rereading until what you recite makes sense and is clear to you in relation to the chapter as a whole. Although you will be doing this step in your head, it's a good idea to practice it in writing a few times first.

EXERCISE
Use the section of this text you just read to answer the following questions:

Title of text _____

Title of chapter _____

Title of major heading _____

What did the author say you must learn? _____

_____

How was it said (i.e., main idea and details, cause and effect argument, descriptive process, case studies, etc.)? _____

_____

_____

Now go over the same exercise using other sections of this text (or any other text you select).

Title of text _____

Title of chapter _____

Title of major heading _____

What did the author say you must learn? _____

_____

How was it said (i.e., main idea and details, cause and effect argument, descriptive process, case studies, etc.)? _____

_____

_____

Title of text _____

Title of chapter _____

Title of major heading _____

What did the author say you must learn? _____

_____

How was it said (i.e., main idea and details, cause and effect argument, descriptive process, case studies, etc.)? _____

_____

_____

Title of text _____

Title of chapter _____

Title of major heading _____

What did the author say you must learn? _____

_____

How was it said (i.e., main idea and details, cause and effect argument, descriptive process, case studies, etc.)? _____

_____

_____

Step 4: Retain the Content

Once you've determined what important information you want to remember, mark it in one of the ways described in the next section of this chapter: note-taking, underlining, charting, or flash cards.

The method you use will be determined by the nature of the material. Use the method most appropriate to the course, the book, and the test. Don't rely on any one method, but learn them all so that you can select the one best suited to your needs. For example, a sequence of events in history might best be noted in outline form, while comparative data on historians or historical events might best be noted in a classification chart.

Step 5: Recite the Content

In order to round off your studying and provide some insurance against memory loss, allow a few minutes at the end of each session with your text to recite. This means going over the material you read and saying it out loud. Use the headings and subheadings of the chapter, either from the book or from your notes. This will depend on whether you've underlined or taken notes on the headings from the chapter. You want to be able to recite as much of the content as possible, checking yourself by looking at the notes, underlining, or using charts after you recite from each section.

Step 6: Review the Content

Once you've read it, noted it, and recited it, frequent review of your underlined text or notes will help you recall the material as well as keep you prepared for exams.

RETAINING TEXT MATERIAL

It was mentioned earlier in the section on note-taking that there are several approaches to noting the material you select for retention from a text chapter: note-taking, underlining, flash cards, and classification charts. Learn them all so that you will have a variety of weapons in your study arsenal. Which one you use will depend on the nature of the content, your particular learning style, and the time available to you. Obviously, whichever form of note-taking you use, it should be done immediately after your first reading of the chapter. The notes represent a permanent record from which you can study any time during the term. The more you review, the easier it is to retain the material and prepare for a test.

Note-taking

Note-taking is a written record of what you select for remembering from the material in a text chapter.

In order to select the material for your notes, it is best to read one section of the text at a time, as explained in step 3, and then ask yourself the two questions stated there: What did the author say that I need to remember? How did the author say it?

The answer to the first question will tell you *what* to write down; the answer to the second, *how* to write it down.

Note-taking can be done in several formats, including outlining and summarizing. Regardless of the format you select, you must remember to use the organization of the chapter to organize your notes. Since most texts have headings at the beginning of each section, use these headings to label the content of your notes. For example, if you take notes on this

chapter, they should reflect the following headings to this point: _____

_____

_____

_____

_____

_____

_____

_____

_____

_____

Another important thing to remember is neatness in note-taking. Just as in lecture note-taking, leave a wide margin at the left of the page as well as a lot of blank space for ease of reading when you go back to study the information. Make your headings stand out from the body of the notes. Wall-to-wall book notes are as poor a study guide as wall-to-wall lecture notes.

Summarizing

Note-taking by summarizing means putting what you must remember in paragraph form. It is best done when the material represents ideas, when the author is repetitious, or when the material is familiar or is common knowledge. Basic types of information such as opinions, beliefs, and points of view are best noted by summarizing. Go back to Chapter 2 and reread the section on Place of Study. Summarize the ideas and write your summary below. Check your notes against Example 5.5, which is in summary form.

Put your summary notes here.

EXAMPLE

5.5

Sample summary notes

Where you study is important in relation to how well you concentrate. A good place means a good physical environment to which you return on a regular basis to achieve the purpose you set for yourself for a particular study session.

Practice by reading sections of this text or any other text and take summary notes on appropriate content material. Make sure your notes reflect the main point being made in the selection as well as some specific supporting details.

Outlining

Note-taking by outlining means putting what you must remember in brief, coordinated form. Use outlining when the material represents related facts and ideas. Basic types of information such as chronological or historical sequences and hierarchies of events or scientific processes are best noted by outlining.

Regardless of the content, good outlining includes:

- Noting the same type of information in each unit of the outline. This means that each statement should contain only one thought, and all the thoughts under a topic should relate to that topic and no other.

- Noting in a consistent form by indentation so that when the outline is gone over, all the main ideas are together in one line and all the subpoints are together in another.

- Using a consistent set of symbols to indicate main ideas and supporting details. If you begin with capital letters for main ideas and numbers for subideas, you must follow through on this for the entire set of outline notes.

EXAMPLE

5.6
Sample outline notes illustrating good form

Chapter 3—Religious Cults—Witchcraft

A. Contemporary Witchcraft
  1. Beliefs
     a. magic—through willpower
     b. contact with the beyond possible
     c. don't harm anyone
     d. reincarnation
     e. power of thought
  2. Rituals
     a. meet at full moon
     b. 4 major sabbaths—4 minor sabbaths
        1. Major Sabbaths

Major sabbaths revolve around "peak" events.

        (a) Halloween—death of old year (Oct. 31)
        (b) Candlemas—initiation of new witches (Feb. 2)
        (c) May Eve—festival of high strength (Apr. 30)
        (d) Lammas—harvest celebration (Aug. 2)
        2. Minor Sabbaths

Minor sabbaths revolve around seasonal changes.

        (a) Winter Solstice—sun's birthday (Dec. 21)
        (b) Spring Equinox—revival of life (Mar. 21)
        (c) Summer Solstice—celebrates power of women (June 21)
        (d) Autumn Equinox—bringing in of crops (Sept. 21)

Look at the sample set of outline notes taken from part of a chapter on various religious cults (Example 5.6). Note that there is consistency of information in each unit of the outline and that the form of indentation and the symbols are uniform throughout. Also note the marginal editing, which can be done for book notes as well as lecture notes.

Look at the following passage from a biology text (Example 5.7). Read it and outline the material on a separate sheet of paper. Compare your outline with Example 5.8. Be sure to read the entire passage first and decide on the information you want to include, making sure it is consistent with the kind of information given in each unit of the outline and that it is indented for ease of reading.

Read sections of this or any other text and practice outline note-taking on the appropriate content material. Make sure each section of the outline notes reflects a large idea presented in the passage, followed by the appropriate supporting details placed beneath it.

EXAMPLE

5.7
Passage from a text

Effects of Distribution of Organisms

There are many other examples of introductions of species, some with good consequences, some with bad consequences. We generally consider the introduction of horses and cattle into the western hemisphere beneficial. Some introductions thought at first to be beneficial turned sour; carp were introduced to the United States from Germany as food fish. They turned out not to be popular with fishers and to interfere with populations of sportfish and waterfowl. The mongoose was introduced from India to Jamaica to control rats and ended up eating almost everything, including chickens, eggs, lambs, kittens, and puppies. Large African grazing mammals such as the kudu have recently been introduced to the United States and Mexico; only time will tell whether they turn out to be beneficial in their new environment. Organisms are often thoughtlessly introduced by people who bring them back from abroad or who release pets they are tired of. The giant African land snail has been introduced into Hawaii, Ceylon, and other Pacific areas, where it devours crops with abandon. The walking catfish from Asia escaped from a pet dealer in Florida; it can move across dry land when its ponds dry up, is reported to be dangerous to dogs and cats, and has invaded swimming pools. The gypsy moth was accidentally released in Massachusetts in 1867; since, it has ravaged vegetation and has been a major cause of DDT use in the United States.

(*Source:* P. R. Ehrlich, R. W. Holm, and I. Brown, *Biology and Society*, McGraw-Hill, 1976. p. 146.).

EXAMPLE

5.8
Outline of

Effects of Introduction of Organisms
into Other Regions

A. Consequences of introduction of species into new regions can be either good or bad.
  1. Horses and cattle
    a. brought to western hemisphere
    b. basically beneficial
  2. Carp
    a. brought to U.S. from Germany
    b. good as food, but not good for fishers or fish populations
  3. Mongoose
    a. brought from India to Jamaica
    b. ended up eating good things (chickens, pets)
  4. African kudu
    a. brought to U.S. and Mexico from Africa
    b. need time to tell if beneficial or not
  5. African land snail
    a. brought in carelessly to Hawaii, Ceylon
    b. eats crops
  6. Walking catfish from Asia
    a. released from a pet store in Florida
    b. eats pets, invades pools
  7. Gypsy moth
    a. accidentally released in Mass.—1867
    b. ravages vegetation

Underlining

Underlining is another extremely useful study skills tool; however, it is frequently underused or misused by students.

Many students don't underline because throughout elementary and high school they have been told not to write in their books. (Libraries tend to frown on it, as a matter of fact.) Also, no one has ever taught them the skill. Now the student has books of his or her own and feels ashamed to write in them; even if it were possible, the student lacks the knowledge of how to do it.

Just as many students misuse the skill. Although they are comfortable with the thought of writing in a book, some students are unsure of how to do it and subsequently wind up underlining too much or too little.

It is safe to say that approximately 30 percent of a chapter represents ideas worth noting and remembering.

Underlining is an important tool because it:

- Promotes interest in the material being read. The reader always has a pen or pencil in hand while reading, and this forces concentration and the sifting out of major ideas and relevant details in order to do the underlining.

- Forces recitation of the material being read before underlining takes place. This allows the student to check out comprehension by saying the ideas aloud. Recitation in the form of review is fostered by going over the underlining after it is done to check it for consistency and accuracy.

- Allows the student to return to the source, the text itself. If things don't make sense, the student can always read around the underlining for clarification.

Some people feel that underlining is only a matter of locating and learning the author's words verbatim rather than putting the ideas into other words. With proper underlining, this isn't so. Let's look at the rules for underlining to find out why.

Rules for Underlining

We will look at five of the more important rules for underlining.

1. *Read the whole selection* (one paragraph, one section, or even an entire chapter) *before underlining*. Most students underline while they read. This is like driving and reading the road map at the same time. You have to know the terrain before you can mark it out. As in step 3 of the text study system, read part of the chapter and then ask yourself the two important questions about content and style.

2. *Recite the ideas you wish to underline in your own words*. This is the result of answering the question, What does the author say?

3. *Underline enough words and phrases from the selection to formulate your own sentences*. In other words, try not to underline complete sentences. However, in the case of important definitions, this may be necessary.

4. *Edit your underlining as you edit class notes*. As long as you're writing in the book, use the margin to organize, summarize, outline, and edit your underlining for ease in studying.

5. *Recite and review the material you underlined at the end of each text-reading session and cumulatively review what you read and underlined each week in every course*. Immediate review promotes retention, and weekly review facilitates learning for testing purposes.

First look at the two samples of underlining below and read only the underlined portions. One paragraph (Example 5.9) is obviously underlined too much, the other (Example 5.10) too little. In one case, it is like reading the whole section over again; in the other case, you'd have to read the

EXAMPLE

5.9
Sample paragraph with too much underlining

Engage in a Job Interview

Once you have gone through the first four steps of securing a job, you are ready to take the final step—the personal interview. This interview is very important to you, because it is here that a final determination is generally made about offering you the position you are applying for. You may have been selected for a personal interview based on your application letter and resumé. Many applicants are not invited for an interview because of poor application letters and resumés. So you have won half the battle.

The personal interview is a two-way communication process and has two purposes. First, it gives the prospective employer the opportunity to meet you and to talk with you. This enables the employer to help decide whether you will fit into the office organization. Second, it gives you the opportunity to consider whether this company is one that you would want to work for.

Be sure to learn all you can about the company before you go for the interview. Know the products or services it sells and whether it is an independent firm or a chain organization. Have some idea of the size of the company, whether it is regional or national, and something about its history and growth. Your knowledge about the firm is evidence to the interviewer that you are really interested in the position.

(*Source:* J. R. Stewart, W. A. Blockhus, C. E. Reigel, and B. L. Schroeder, *Office Procedures*, McGraw-Hill, 1980, p. 431).

section again because when too few words are underlined, the sense of the material gets lost.

Now look at the same passage underlined correctly (Example 5.11). Enough words and phrases are marked so that the meaning of the section comes through when they are reread. It's just the right amount of information necessary for recall. Also notice the aids used to make the information visible. The words "first" and "second" are circled to call your attention to a list of points. In the last paragraph, the points are numbered for the same purpose. The marginal notes index the material for easy studying. Edit your underlining the same way you edit lecture notes.

Practice your underlining techniques on the content passages used as examples in this section, on other sections of this text, or on any other text material you have. Read the passage and then put what it says in your own words. Then underline it. Be patient. Underlining is a tricky skill to acquire, but the results are well worth the effort. Reread only the underlined part in each of your practice passages, checking it to make

EXAMPLE

5.10
Sample paragraph with too little underlining

Engage in a Job Interview

Once you have gone through the first four steps of securing a job, you are ready to take the final step—the personal interview. This interview is very important to you, because it is here that a final determination is generally made about offering you the position you are applying for. You may have been selected for a personal interview based on your application letter and résumé. Many applicants are not invited for an interview because of poor application letters and résumés. So you have won half the battle.

The personal interview is a two-way communication process and has two purposes. First, it gives the prospective employer the opportunity to meet you and to talk with you. This enables the employer to help decide whether you will fit into the office organization. Second, it gives you the opportunity to consider whether this company is one that you would want to work for.

Be sure to learn all you can about the company before you go for the interview. Know the products or services it sells and whether it is an independent firm or a chain organization. Have some idea of the size of the company, whether it is regional or national, and something about its history and growth. Your knowledge about the firm is evidence to the interviewer that you are really interested in the position.

EXAMPLE

5.11
Paragraph underlined correctly

Engage in a Job Interview

personal interview

2 purposes: you talk to them, they talk to you

Once you have gone through the first four steps of securing a job, you are ready to take the final step—the personal interview. This interview is very important to you, because it is here that a final determination is generally made about offering you the position you are applying for. You may have been selected for a personal interview based on your application letter and résumé. Many applicants are not invited for an interview because of poor application letters and résumés. So you have won half the battle.

The personal interview is a two-way communication process and has two purposes. First, it gives the prospective employer the opportunity to

EXAMPLE

5.11
Continued.

Know about company before you go there.

meet you and to talk with you. This enables the employer to help decide whether you will fit into the office organization. Second, it gives you the opportunity to consider whether this company is one that you would want to work for.

Be sure to learn all you can about the company before you go for the interview. Know the products or services it sells and whether it is an independent firm or a chain organization. Have some idea of the size of the company, whether it is regional or national, and something about its history and growth. Your knowledge about the firm is evidence to the interviewer that you are really interested in the position.

sure you noted the important ideas. Make any marginal notes you feel would assist you in reciting and reviewing the material.

Flash Cards

Chances are, you used flash cards as a study method back in elementary school for learning multiplication tables or for drilling yourself on spelling or vocabulary words in English or a foreign language.

Many college courses involve the remembering of large amounts of isolated information, such as vocabulary words, formulas, equations, definitions, dates, names, or questions. As a matter of fact, introductory courses in most basic science and social science areas, such as biology, elementary psychology, and political science, are overwhelmingly based on vocabulary items. Flash cards are a great way to learn them.

Some advantages of this method are:

- Writing the cards is an aid to memory, since you can recite and review as you prepare the cards.

- They can be carried conveniently and reviewed frequently throughout the day. Using spare bits of time to review flash cards can net you many valuable study hours over the course of a week. Remember, study skills research reveals that short reviews spaced out over time are generally more effective than long sessions or cramming.

- Flash cards, unlike notes, can be shuffled to ensure that learning will not be in a sequence but in random order. Cards can also be grouped according to ideas. For example, in an anatomy class, all the cards relating to major muscle groups or blood types can be separated to show yourself that you recognize which items belong with which categories.

Some suggestions for making flash cards:

- Use 3 by 5 cards, either commercially prepared or paper you cut to size.

- Put the term, equation, rule, or data on one side and a definition, explanation, or example on the other.

- Self-test frequently in short study sessions, making sure to shuffle the cards so as not to learn them in any one order.

- Break the cards up into category groupings.

- Overlearn the cards by going through them two or three times after you are able to do one perfect recitation.

- Prepare and study the cards daily and weekly rather than just before a test so that test preparation is a reviewing process rather than a learning and memorizing process.

Here are some examples of the different types of note cards:

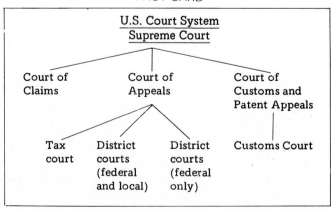

VOCABULARY CARD

| Ability | The potential a person has for acquiring a skill, i. e. intelligence or aptitude to perform a specific skill. |

Front   Back

FACT CARD

U.S. Court System
Supreme Court

Court of Claims Court of Appeals Court of Customs and Patent Appeals

Tax court District courts (federal and local) District courts (federal only) Customs Court

EQUATION CARD

Finding the mean of a frequency distribution $$\overline{X} = \dfrac{E \times f}{N}$$	$\overline{X}$ = mean of a F.D. E = sum of the scores f = frequency N = # in sample **The mean of a frequency distribution is equal to the sum of the scores times the frequency divided by the number in the sample.**
Front	Back

Example 5.12 is a section from a psychology chapter. Read it and prepare vocabulary and fact flash cards for the purpose of studying the material. A few samples of the possible note cards that can be constructed from it are given below.

EXAMPLE

5.12

   Variables   As the term implies, a variable is an event or condition which can have different values. Ideally, it is an event or condition which can be measured and which varies quantitatively.

   Variables may be either independent or dependent. An independent variable is a condition set or a set selected by an experimenter to see whether it will have an effect on behavior; it might be a stimulus presented, a drug administered, a new method of training business managers, and so on. The dependent variable is the behavior of a person or animal in an experiment. A dependent variable in an experiment might be the response of a person to a stimulus, a change in behavior after the administration of a drug, changes in managerial behavior after a new training program has been instituted, a score on a test, a verbal report about an event in the environment, and so on. The dependent variable is so called because its value depends, or may depend, on the value of the independent variable—the one independently chosen and directly manipulated by the experimenter.

   When, in doing experiments, hypotheses are formulated about the effect of one thing or another, the independent variable is the one expected to produce changes in the dependent variable. Consider the following hypotheses, for instance: Enriching the environments of young children with special

EXAMPLE

5.12
Continued.

books and toys will increase their scores on intelligence tests; giving people training in how to meditate will improve their skill as tennis players. The environmental enrichment and the meditation training are the independent variables, while the changes in intelligence test scores and tennis skills (possible outcomes of differences in the independent variables) are the dependent variables. When you read accounts of psychological or other experiments, it is essential that you distinguish the independent and dependent variables clearly.

In graphing the results of an experiment, it is conventional in psychology to plot values of the independent variable on the horizontal axis, or abscissa, and values of the dependent variable on the vertical axis, or ordinate. Thus we can see at a glance how the dependent variable of behavior is related to values of the independent variable (Figure 1.7).

(*Source:* C. T. Morgan, R. A. King, and N. M. Robinson, *Introduction to Psychology*, 6th ed., McGraw-Hill, 1979, p. 20.)

Sample Flash Cards Made from Psychology Passage

VOCABULARY CARD

Variable	Event or condition which varies and can be measured

Front   Back

VOCABULARY CARD

Hypotheses	Ideas about the possible effect of one variable on another

Front   Back

FACT CARD

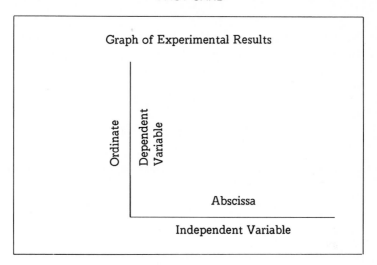

Practice making flash cards on sections of this text or any other material you may have that would be appropriate for this kind of note-taking.

Organizational Tables

Organizational tables help classify or summarize material to reflect similarities, differences, or relationships between two or more items.

No doubt you have seen organizational tables in a variety of reading materials. They appear frequently in textbooks, but they are also used in newspaper and magazine articles when the author wishes to clarify confusing information. Text authors use them to graphically summarize or classify information presented in the body of a chapter. A long section or whole chapter devoted to discussing the relationship between the ideas of several experts or researchers, or the relationship between two or more events or processes, can be condensed for ease of understanding. In the same way, newspapers and magazines use such tables to accompany the narrative in order to show the relationship between the stands of political candidates, the allocation of funds among states, or the relationship between the borrowing habits of underdeveloped nations and their inability to repay the debts incurred.

Organizational tables are valuable in almost all content areas. They are best used when outlining or underlining would not be appropriate. Usually the material is comparative in nature and heavily factual. If you underlined, it would probably result in too many markings; if you outlined

EXAMPLE

5.13
Sample organizational chart

Rituals (Sabbaths)

NAME OF SABBATH	MAJOR SABBATHS				MINOR SABBATHS			
	HALLOWEEN	CANDLEMAS	MAY EVE	LAMMAS	WINTER SOLSTICE	SPRING EQUINOX	SUMMER SOLSTICE	AUTUMN EQUINOX
DATE OF SABBATH	OCT. 31	FEB. 2	APR. 30	AUG. 2	DEC. 21	MAR. 21	JUNE 21	SEPT. 21
Purpose of sabbath	Death of old year—dress up so people can't find you. Equal to All Saints' Day in Catholic church.	Initiation of new witches.	Festival of high strength.	Harvest celebration.	Sun's birthday. Equal to Dec. 25 in Catholic church.	Revival of life festival.	Strength of women celebrated.	Celebration of the harvest.

(probably possible due to the nature of the material), you would not see the comparisons as well.

Look back at the outline notes from the section on witchcraft on page 95. It is concerned with the basic beliefs of the witches and their eight sabbaths. For each sabbath a date is given, along with the general nature of the celebration. Even though it is clear and concise, it is still hard to see the relationship among the various rituals. Since the same material is given for all eight rituals, it is also possible to chart the information. From which would you rather study, the outline or the chart in Example 5.13?

The most important aspect of making a table is labeling. After reading the passage or chapter and deciding that a table would be the best way to note the material, ask yourself what things are being compared or contrasted or what the likenesses or differences are between them.

Let's look at a sampling of organizational tables from material in a variety of courses. Health, nutrition, and nursing classes contain a lot of factual material that is easily organized into tables for clarity of comprehension.

In any of the classes mentioned above, nutrients are usually discussed. The text passages are heavily factual, but the same basic topics are related to each nutrient. Underlining is not the best method of noting the material because it is too factual, and outlining is not as useful for seeing relationships. A table labeled like the one below would best display the information and provide a ready guide for studying and predicting exam questions.

Vitamin	A	B	C	D	E	K
Food sources						
Other sources						
Effects on individuals from too much						
Effects on individuals from too little						

Nutrients—Vitamins

In nursing programs, the same material is applied to the varied diseases discussed. A table laying out the material in an organized fashion might look like this:

Chronic diseases	Disease 1	Disease 2	Disease 3	Disease 4
Causes				
Descriptors				
Patient behavior if condition worsens				
Nursing actions				
Medications				

A course in the humanities covering many periods of time, but covering similar material for each era, is fine subject matter for a table. For example, in a music survey course, you might organize the material as shown in the table on the facing page.

	Renaissance	Baroque	Classical	Romantic	Contemporary
Dates of period					
Major musical styles of period					
Major composers of period					
Major exemplary works of period					
Social, political, and historical events of period					

Turn to page 218 in the section on social science study techniques. Read the passage on the workings of Congress and formulate an organizational table on the content. Then turn to Example 5.14 and compare the results.

Continue to practice making organizational charts on material from this book or any other appropriate material.

EXAMPLE

5.14
Organizational table for sample paragraph

	Senate	House of Representatives
Structure	800 members—size and structure permits informal procedures with all being consulted.	Larger—so structure is tighter—strict rules—work done with careful division of labor.
Power	Evenly distributed— Everyone on at least one major committee. Are in national limelight.	Lower profile—more dependent on seniors in House to attain power—so more need to conform.
Knowledge and work load	Heavy committee schedules means reliance on others for specialized knowledge.	Greater number means more equal share of work load—can specialize in particular subject areas.

Summary

— Text reading constitutes one of the major aspects of academic work.
— To understand what you read, it is necessary to be aware of how texts are organized as well as how the chapters and paragraphs are arranged.
— Use a systematic approach to a text chapter: Preview it, read it, locate and state the ideas presented, retain the content in the method most appropriate (by outlining, underlining, making flash cards, or making organizational tables), and finally recite and review frequently to ensure retention for test-taking.

6 | **PREPARING FOR EXAMINATIONS**

This chapter is concerned with preparing for exams. It suggests that exam preparation is a four-step process: examining the exam, examining yourself, predicting what is going to be on the exam from the course content, and finally, self-testing in order to learn the material. It strongly urges that in order to be an active learner, you must learn to do self-questioning in preparation for the exam. Several different types of questions that can be used in practice are presented.

Mentally review the strategies you have used in preparation for exams. Complete the following statement.

In general, when I prepare for an exam _____

_____

_____

_____

Therefore, based on your experience, in order to get the most out of this

chapter, the information you will want to concentrate on will be _____

_____

_____

_____

As we said in Chapter 2, exams are really not cruel and excessive punishment but a good way for both the instructor and you to evaluate how you are doing in a course.

Throughout this book, we have stressed the need for you to stay caught up in your course work, and nowhere does it pay off better than in preparing for and taking exams. Being caught up means having read and reviewed all the assigned reading material on time, having edited and reviewed all the lecture notes on a regular basis, and having completed all outside assignments such as worksheets and papers.

Working under these conditions means you can begin to study for an exam several days (or perhaps a week) before it occurs, and you can still keep up with your other courses since you will not have to sacrifice whole days and nights, giving your attention only to the subject on which you are about to be tested. Students who spend all their time before an exam on only one subject agree that the penalty is getting further behind in their other courses. If it seems like a circular process, it is. You, however, are the one caught in the middle, running in that evertightening circle.

Exam preparation can be broken down into four stages: examining the exam, examining yourself, figuring out and organizing what is going to be on the exam, and, finally, learning the material.

Each time you get ready to study for a test, you can mentally (or on paper) go through the steps in the process. It won't be necessary to start at the beginning each time. If you are in the great state of being caught up, you will probably be ready to begin at step 3. If you are not, it probably will mean going back to the drawing board again. If some of the topics that were on the midquarter appear on the final, you probably will be able to skip ahead to step 4.

STEP 1: EXAMINING THE EXAM

Before you begin to study for an exam, you have to know what to expect when you get to the testing situation. Information about the exams comes from a variety of sources: the syllabus, the instructor, friends and other students who have had the course before you, and earlier tests in the same class. If you don't have any of this information, your job is easy—ask. Ask the instructor, ask a friend, ask your counselor, or ask in the library or skills center. It is possible that one of these two places keeps copies of old exams on file for students to look at and use as guidelines for studying. Going to a test not knowing what to expect will lessen the chances of being able to do your best.

Here are some of the things you will want to know beforehand and what they will mean to you as you prepare for an exam.

First of all, what kind of test will it be: objective, short answer, essay, or problem solving? For an objective test, you will probably have to learn more facts. For an essay exam, you will have to be able to use the facts that you know to construct a well-thought-out answer to the questions asked.

You will be interested to know that regardless of the type of test, research indicates that students who study as if every test they took were an essay exam do better on both essay and objective tests. The moral is: If you don't know what type of test it will be, study as if it were going to be an essay test.

What sources will be covered on the test and to what depth? Will the material from the text be stressed, or the material from the lecture notes, or perhaps both? Knowing the emphasis of the test will help you determine how to spend your study time.

How much time was spent on the various topics covered in the course? Will the topics that were covered in the greatest depth be the ones stressed on the test? This is an area in which students sometimes get into trouble, the reason being that a student might think that since a topic was only gone into briefly, it won't appear or count for much on the test. Since this isn't necessarily the case, don't be fooled. If you have any questions as to the weight of a topic in relation to a test, *ask* the instructor. You won't necessarily get a straight or even a complete answer, but you may get enough of a clue to help you decide how much time to spend studying a particular topic.

Once you have an idea of the topics to be covered, you can think about the kinds of questions that may be asked about them. Do you think the questions will require you to know and recall many facts, such as names, terms, dates, or vocabulary items? Or will the questions require you to put together ideas and explain, illustrate, apply, or evaluate the information?

How many questions will there be on the test? Many multiple-choice questions covering relatively few topics probably means that it will be necessary for you to learn the material in great depth. Two essay questions covering a whole term's work probably means that it will be necessary for you to have a broad general understanding of the material.

You will also want to know how much time you will have for the test. Thirty-five or forty multiple-choice questions in a fifty-minute exam means that there is little time to think about each answer, while two essay questions in fifty minutes means that you will have time to think in order to construct a good answer.

In an essay test, you will want to find out the biases of the people grading the test. Do they take points off for inaccurate spelling, grammatically incorrect sentences, or essays without introductions and conclusions?

Finally, you will want to find out what weight the test carries in determining your grade. Obviously, exams in a course with only a midquarter and final carry more weight than exams in courses where there are weekly quizzes and other frequent means of evaluation. If you are taking more than one course, knowing the weight of an exam in determining your grade will help you decide where to spend the most study time.

STEP 2: EXAMINING YOURSELF

What is your reaction when you think about an upcoming exam? Panic? Avoidance of the problem? Cramming? Perhaps exams make you think of long days and nights spent in hard work for which you receive little payoff in the form of a good grade. Can you think of the best exam experience you ever had? How did you handle it? What was the payoff like?

Whatever experiences you may have had, adequate planning for an exam requires that you take a look at yourself. Begin by asking yourself where you are in relation to the course. What is the state of your preparedness for studying? Are you caught up in your reading? Are your notes all edited? Are your assignments all completed?

If you are not caught up, make a list of what you have to do (pages to read, problems to solve). This should help you decide how to spend your time before the exam. Obviously, if the test is based on your lecture notes and they are not complete, it would be wise to get notes from someone else and fill in the gaps. If the test is based on the text, you may have to skim the material rather than read slowly and intensively, word by word. Chapter summaries and key ideas from chapter headings are probably all you will have time for. Cutting corners at this time should be based on existing conditions, what you know will be on the test, and the time remaining before the test; it should not be based on a hit-or-miss process of elimination.

Think about where you are in relation to a course in which you are now enrolled and are about to be tested. What would you have to do to be caught up if you were to have a test one week from today, three days from now, or tomorrow?

If you are not enrolled in a course at present, you can apply the exercise to any goals on which you happen to be working. What would you have to do to get caught up if the target date for completion were one week away, three days away, or tomorrow?

After you have figured out what there is to do and the time remaining in which to do it, you will want to work it into your study schedule.

Course	Where I am	What I would do if a test were		
		1 week away	3 days away	Tomorrow

What did you learn by filling in the chart? _____

_____

In some courses instructors, give surprise, or pop, tests. How would you do if you were tested today in any of your classes? _____

_____

What changes would you have to make in your study strategies to be in a position where a pop test would cause you no problems at all? _____

_____

This is a good place to talk about time-scheduling and exam preparation. It is not too different from time-scheduling in general, except that the questions are a little different. Begin by asking yourself how much time there is before the test and what you have to do to get ready. Be sure to include all your regular obligations, such as reading, writing for other courses, work and class hours, and all the other things that can't be put off. You will see how much time remains for study. Look for hidden time, such as breaks at work and intervals between classes. Be sure to include some time for friends and exercise. Unwinding and relaxing are very important at exam time.

If you have an exam coming up, you will want to use the accompanying chart to figure out a new schedule for the days just before the test. Based on where you are in your preparation and what remains to be done, how will you spend your time?

Another thing to consider is your ability in relation to the kind of test being given. What kind of test is it going to be, and what has your

Time Analysis for week of _____

	Mon.	Tues.	Wed.	Thurs.	Fri.	Sat.	Sun.
7 A.M.							
8 A.M.							
9 A.M.							
10 A.M.							
11 A.M.							
12 –							
1 P.M.							
2 P.M.							
3 P.M.							
4 P.M.							
5 P.M.							
6 P.M.							
7 P.M.							
8 P.M.							
9 P.M.							
10 P.M.							
11 P.M.							
12 –							
1 A.M.							

Pre-exam time schedule

performance ability been like on similar tests in the past? _____

This information can help you determine the areas to stress in your studying. For example, did you not have enough facts the last time you wrote an essay exam? Or did you have too many facts and not enough concepts when you took an objective test? Is it a kind of test you have never had before? If so, you may need to ask or read about strategies for preparation and test-taking in the new situation.

In considering your personal reactions to exams, it is important to note that many students change their entire life patterns at exam time. This can be hazardous to both your mental and physical well-being. If you spend endless hours studying, avoiding friends, and eating hastily put together meals of high-calorie foods such as fries, shakes, and candy bars, combined with little sleep and exercise, you are bound to pay a price. Putting the possible weight gain aside, you will become tired more quickly and will resent the very books and notes you need to study for the exam. You probably will spend more time psyching yourself up for studying than in the actual act of studying.

The lesson is that if you are caught up, you can study and maintain an almost normal life pattern. Your usual social, physical, and mental self is left pretty much intact rather than in a state of total disruption.

STEP 3: DETERMINING WHAT'S GOING TO BE ON THE EXAM

In many of the preceding chapters, stress was placed on organization, a key element in studying. In this step in the exam preparation process, organization again becomes an important ingredient of success.

Exams cover many topics and much material. What to study for a test and the best methods for remembering are the subjects of this section.

Once you know the basis of the test—that is, the text, the notes, or perhaps both—the task becomes one of going through your books or notes and developing an outline of all the topics and subtopics sure to be on the test. For example, the table of contents of the text can serve as a perfect outline if the exam is based on the book. Your well-edited notes should yield such a list if notes are the most important element. A combination of both would be appropriate if material from both text and notes will be on the test. In some cases, an instructor will provide the information for you, either verbally before the test or on the course syllabus.

The longer the time between exams, the bigger the list. There may be only four or five topics on a midquarter but perhaps as many as ten or twelve on a final.

Once you have a list of the topics to be covered on the test, you can reflect on how well you understand them. It is at this point that you should go back and reread a part of the text which you feel is unfamiliar or learn how to solve a problem, the solution to which you are unsure.

If you have trouble deciding which topic to study first or second, ask yourself what you would study and how you would spend your time if you only had one day, sixty minutes, or thirty minutes left before a test.

Suppose you were to have a multiple-choice test on the first five chapters or whatever you have read in this book to date. List the major topics and the related subtopics which you assume would be on such a test.

Major topic _____   Major topic _____

Subtopics _____   Subtopics _____

_____   _____

Major topic _____   Major topic _____

Subtopics _____   Subtopics _____

_____   _____

What information would you have to review before beginning to study

for the exam? _____

_____

Go through the same process for any course in which an exam is fast approaching.

Major topic _____   Major topic _____

Subtopics _____   Subtopics _____

_____   _____

Major topic _____   Major topic _____

Subtopics _____   Subtopics _____

_____   _____

What information would you have to review before beginning to study

for the exam? _____

Ways to Organize

Once you have decided what will be on the test, the next step involves how to remember it. Once again, organization is the key element. The human mind does not do well trying to remember a series of disconnected facts. Take the following list of items that can be found in any supermarket:

milk	butter	hamburger
green beans	eggplant	cheese
cabbage	noodles	mushrooms
juice	salt	broccoli
lamb chops	soup	chicken
cauliflower	eggs	lettuce
vinegar	beef	cottage cheese
pepper	sour cream	mayonnaise

Read through the list several times and try to recite it correctly. How long did it take you to complete one perfect recitation?

Most people would have to go over the list many times in order to recall the items accurately and in the right order; if they tried to recite it again after only a day, they would have forgotten more than half the items.

This kind of learning, called rote learning, is similar to what happens when you study merely by reviewing your notes, reading them through from top to bottom several times. If your memory fails on a test, you would have to scan your notes mentally, starting at the beginning. Many students who study this way say they can see the information and where it is on a particular page in their text or notebook but are unable to retrieve it to answer the test question. Sound familiar?

However, if you organize or, more correctly, categorize the information, as in the supermarket list, remembering increases dramatically. If you take the items and organize them by topic and then study them, you will see how easily you can remember them.

Look at the categories and enter each item from the list under the proper heading:

Meat items	Dairy items	Vegetable items	Grocery items

Take time to learn the items in their proper categories. How long did it take you to complete one perfect recitation this time?

Let's apply this to your studying. Here are a few ways you can organize material for an exam in order to both study and remember it.

FLASH CARDS

Flash cards can be used to learn specific facts or general principles. Factual flash cards can be made for vocabulary words, formulas, theorems or equations, definitions, and dates or names. General principle flash cards can be made for main ideas, lists of characteristics, cause and effect relationships, chronological lists, and groups of terms. Review the types of flash cards and the rules for making them from the note-taking section of Chapter 5.

The student who is caught up makes flash cards as new terms, ideas, or formulas are introduced throughout the course. There is a benefit in just making them, since writing the cards is an aid to memory. Because they are small and brief, they can be carried everywhere and reviewed often, and they can be broken down into small learning units.

KEY POINTS OUTLINES

This technique is especially useful when you have several sources of information for one topic. In other words, you develop an outline or summary of key points for a topic from several sources: the book, your notes, outside reading, etc. They may be made on paper or large note cards and carried around for frequent, easy recitation and review. A key points outline would look like this.

KEY POINT	BOOK	LECTURE NOTES	OUTSIDE SOURCE
Behaviorism	Began with Watson and the study of behavior rather than the mind. Also emphasizes conditioned responses, learned rather than unlearned behavior, and differences between human and animal behavior.	Examples of conditioned behavior— Pavlov and dog experiments B. F. Skinner only concerned with what one can see and how it is affected by stimuli or rewards.	Article on Skinner Extensive research with animals (rats and pigeons). Experiments are proofs of learned behavior using rewards to shape behavior. Invented teaching machines—one result is programmed books and learning materials.

ORGANIZATIONAL CHARTS

You have seen charts of this type in your other texts and in newspapers and magazines. Writers use them as a way of simplifying difficult material in order to make comparisons and relationships clear to the reader. They can also help you understand and learn the information that might appear on a test. They are appropriate for almost any course. As in the case of flash cards, outlines or charts made before exam preparation are ideal. It is harder, however, since your reading notes may not be complete till right before the test. Review the paragraphs on making organizational charts from the note-taking section of Chapter 5.

STEP 4: SELF-TESTING

Once the exam material has been boiled down for studying, you will want to spend the majority of your time talking to yourself, or self-testing. Recitation and spaced practice are just as important at this stage of studying as when you are reading the text, and the benefits are the same. Look back at Chapter 5 if you have forgotten.

It is important not to learn the information just as it appears on your flash cards, outlines, or charts. The questions on a test are never in the same order in which they appear in your notes. Organizing course content and self-testing allow you to see relationships between topics and discover where your information is inadequate (if you can't fill in a cell on a chart, for instance). It also keeps you alert and thinking about the subject matter. You are actually practicing taking the test, predicting and answering potential exam questions.

For outlines or charts, try to ask yourself questions similar to those which might appear on the test or at least appropriate to the subject matter. Exams, whether objective or subjective, test for both main ideas and supporting facts. Therefore, questions requiring a brief one- or two-word answer won't make you recite enough or force you to go over the course content in a variety of ways. Try to ask yourself brief, essay-type questions. They will make you think about, recite, and turn over the subject matter so that you are comparing, contrasting, and seeing relationships between the ideas and their details.

Beside the obvious review element, at this stage you will want to shuffle the flash cards like any deck of cards, sorting them out by chronological order, relationships, or category. If you have a set of vocabulary cards for anatomy, for instance, each one listing the name of a muscle, nerve, or bone of the body, you may go through them by category (muscle, nerve, or bone), function, or position in the human skeleton.

Most students do not have the questioning habit, mainly because they never learned how. The next section deals with the whys of questions and the various types with which you should be familiar.

Asking Questions

Throughout this book, emphasis has been placed on an active approach to learning. One of the most important techniques that enhances learning is asking questions, which in turn fosters mental manipulation and recitation of the material to be learned. Asking questions about the content is appropriate in many study situations: before hearing a lecture, after a lecture while going over notes, while previewing a chapter before reading, during recitation of the material after reading, and, of course, while studying for an exam.

The question is, Why ask questions? Many students believe that the instructor gives what is supposed to be learned. Therefore, learning is considered a repetition or regurgitation of the material given. *Not so.* Instructors are there *not* to fill your head with knowledge (sometimes called the hole-in-the-head theory of education) but to introduce you to the material they feel is most important in the course or discipline they are teaching. Your job is not to repeat the information but to use it wisely in the process of educating yourself. A good instructor is a guide to the content, ideas, and materials of learning. You are the consumer, taking in the facts and ideas, and comparing, contrasting, classifying, and summarizing it all in order to be able to add it to what you already know and to discover where you possibly want or need to add more knowledge. After all, the more you know about a subject, the easier it is for you to add more knowledge to what is already there—it makes further learning easier.

Some side effects of well-used knowledge include improved understanding, better retention, and increased self-esteem as a student and as a contributing member of the various groups in which you interact every day: social, family, and work.

Studying by questioning becomes a rehearsal of the test situation. A student who knows the course content and the type of test that will be given essentially takes the test before it is given.

There are several basic types of questions you will want to learn to ask in order to be able to study effectively.

Although questions have to be more than a mere repetition of fact, it is sometimes necessary to quiz yourself on straight recall of knowledge previously presented by a lecturer or in your text reading. The first kind of question, then, is one intended to promote straight recall of factural material.

To go beyond the facts, you have to ask yourself questions that force you to verbalize or work with the material, putting it into your words by describing, summarizing, analyzing, tracing, and contrasting and comparing. Any of the terms listed as potential question words for essay exams (Chapter 7) can be used to stimulate and originate questions in this second category. This will give you the ability to apply, criticize, analyze, or evaluate the material for application-type questions on exams.

The accompanying chart takes some basic subject matter and traces it through the formulation of the three basic types of questions that help in the recall of information.

Group Study

At this point you may like the idea of doing some group study—a get-together with several other people in your class after each of you has studied independently. An admission price should be set for each person attending the group session. For example, each participant should be required to bring along a number of questions for the other members of the group to answer.

These sessions can be both stimulating and supporting. You wouldn't want to attend a group study session unless you felt you had studied well on your own first. However, you would know that help is available from the other group members for any problems you had with the subject. Group study is also a good way to get another outlook on the topic.

The drawback, of course, is that a group study session can become a bull session. It is important to select study partners who are serious and task-oriented, committed to getting the studying job done. It helps to impose both a structure and a time limit on a group study session.

RECALLING THE INFORMATION	VERBALIZING THE INFORMATION	USING THE INFORMATION
1. In what year was George Washington born?	Briefly review the major accomplish-ments of his career as a general, as a President	How did his ideas on the formation of the new gov-ernment differ from those of Thomas Jefferson? Benjamin Franklin?
2. Define the term "existentialism" and "behaviorism."	Compare and contrast the two terms.	What are the implications of existentialism and behav-iorism upon human growth and potential?
3. What are the steps in the process of cell reproduction?	Describe the action taking place during each step in the process.	Diagram the process of cell reproduction for both a normal and an abnormal cell and relate the differ-ences between the two.
4. Who fought in the War of 1812, and what were the issues?	Summarize the polit-ical events sur-rounding the period.	In what ways were the political events sur-rounding the War of 1812 similar to/different from those of the Revolutionary War?
5. Who were Thorn-dike, Watson, Pavlov, and Skin-ner? State the major premise of each in relation to their ideas on learn-ing and behavior.	Trace the develop-ment of learning theory from Thorn-dike through Skin-ner, including the differences be-tween them.	How would each theorist explain the following bits of behavior?
6. Where are the Alps located, and what was the geological process which caused their forma-tion?	Describe the process by which the Alps were formed as well as the two other processes by which mountains are formed.	Locate the Alps on the map and provide an example for each of the other types of geological processes.
7. What is a financial statement, and why does a company use one?	What kinds of informa-tion are contained in a financial state-ment, and what is the purpose of each piece of information in relation to the whole thing?	Examine the financial state-ments of several com-panies. What do you know about the companies from reading them? or Construct a financial statement for Company X given the following information.

SUMMARY

—The key to exam preparation is always being caught up so that pre-exam time is a review period, not a relearning period.

—In order to prepare well, you have to know about the particulars of the exam—what kind of test it will be, when it will be given, what will be on it, etc.—as well as yourself—how you stand in relation to being caught up and your personal reactions to the exam.

—Good exam preparation includes knowing what will be on the test, predicting the topics and possible questions in advance, and using appropriate study techniques to organize the material (key points outlines, flash cards, and organizational tables).

—The most important step in exam preparation is self-testing, or asking yourself appropriate questions covering the content you expect to be on the exam.

STRATEGIES FOR TAKING EXAMS | 7

This chapter is concerned with strategies for taking both essay and objective tests. It is broken down into the time periods before, during, and after an exam. General strategies are given for personal gearing up before an exam, and specific strategies are given for taking both types of tests. Testwiseness clues are given for assistance in taking objective tests, and finally, a discussion of, and some practical tips on, exam panic are given.

Mentally review your test-taking experiences and your general attitude toward exams. Complete the following statements:

In general, my experience with tests has been _____

_____

_____

_____

When I know a test is coming, I feel _____

_____

_____

_____

When I am sitting for an exam, I feel _____

_____

_____

_____

Therefore, based on your experience with and feelings about exams, in order to get the most out of this chapter, you will want to pay particular

attention to _____

_____

_____

_____

There are two basic types of exams: (1) subjective or essay, in which the test-taker has to construct the answer to a question, and (2) objective or short answer, in which the test-taker has to recognize or select the correct answer to a question.

Essays vary in length, but most importantly they vary according to the instructional or clue words in the question—your guideline to what is wanted in the way of an answer.

Objective tests vary according to specific types of questions—multiple-choice, true-false, matching, or fill-in-the-blanks.

More specific pointers about each of these appear in the section titled During the Test.

BEFORE THE TEST

The following accumulation of simple strategies should be kept in mind before you take the actual exam.

1. Study well. There is no substitute for proper preparation before an exam for self-esteem, confidence, and the reduction of test anxiety.

2. Sleep well the night before the exam. Remember, sleep is an inhibitor of forgetting. Sleep is a neutral activity as opposed to seeing a movie, watching television, or reading for pleasure or study purposes.

Activities such as reading and studying tend to interfere with both learning and retention. If you read after studying, for example, the new reading activity tends to interfere with the former reading activity and with the retention of the material just learned for a test. The closer the relationship between the two activities, the more the potential confusion. Memorizing terms should not be followed by more memory work but by a different activity, for example, problem solving or writing.

If it is getting late and you are tired, sleep. Get up early in the morning and go over the material again before the exam. This is preferable to staying up late, or all night, before an exam. It certainly won't do you harm to stay up all night. But, recalling what was said about concentration and spaced versus unspaced practice, you should see the wisdom of a good night's sleep before an exam.

3. Attend all class lectures, labs, and discussion sections both during the course and just before a test. You can usually pick up some valuable information on the content or format of a test just before it is given.

4. Get to the test location on time. Arriving too early, say fifteen minutes beforehand, can set up anxiety, especially if classmates are around swapping questions or trying to get information about which they are unsure. Hearing people discuss material on which you feel shaky is not a confidence booster just before an exam.

Arriving too late, say just as the test is being distributed, can also set up anxiety.

Try to arrive just early enough to comfortably settle in to your seat, line up your pens and pencils, and relax.

5. Eat sensibly before an exam—not too much, and certainly don't go into a test without having eaten at all.

Too much food, or too much of the wrong food, such as a large dose of carbohydrates (french fries, malts, etc.) or greasy or acidic foods, can make you ill or tired.

If you are hungry from lack of food, you may spend more time concentrating on your hunger and the noises emanating from your stomach than on the test.

Just the right amount of food means a moderate breakfast or lunch—satisfying but not filling. Save the calorie glut for a reward after successfully completing the test rather than as an antidote against the test.

6. Before exams, try to maintain as normal a life as possible. If you are usually in the habit of taking regular exercise, try to maintain your exercise routine. If you are in the habit of working or socializing, try to maintain as normal a schedule of work and play as possible. Remember, if you have been keeping up throughout the term, exam time is review time, not cram time. If you are behind, it is usually not a good idea psychologically to cut yourself off from all your usual activities. Besides the self-anger created by having to cram and the possible consequences to your course grade, you may build up resentment over the hours you spend at work rather than at study or over being cut off from your friends and family.

If you are the chief caretaker of a household, during exam time you may need a few more hours away from the others, or at least more cooperation in getting chores accomplished. A family conference to explain your needs and the agreed-on delegation of tasks to and by other family members will relieve some of the pressure. This is especially helpful if you have been away from school for a while and the thought of exams has made you somewhat anxious. Family members feel better if they voluntarily select a task from a prepared list rather than arbitrarily being assigned a task.

If each member selects his or her own assignment from a list of things to be done, there is bound to be less of a hassle than if the assignments are made and distributed army-style. Posting the task list on the kitchen refrigerator or on the wallboard, along with a check-off system for recording the completion of the job, keeps everyone alert and aware of his or her responsibilities. Some reward for the helpers at the end of the exam period goes a long way toward getting the chores done with a smile. It may be a specially prepared meal, an outing to a movie or other longed-for activity, or just the knowledge that the heat is off and Mom or Dad is back at the helm once again.

It is hard to do a good job at test preparation and test-taking if you are angry or upset because you either had to do all the household jobs yourself or felt that you had to let them go in favor of the exams.

7. As silly as it sounds, make sure you know when and where an exam is given. Final exams in particular are usually given during a week or other time period set aside just for that purpose. A course exam can be scheduled at an hour and in a room quite different from the time and place of the usual class lecture or lab. Exam schedules are printed in the class schedule for each term and are usually printed in a college publication such as the daily or weekly newspaper just before exam time. Don't depend on your instructor to make sure each student is informed of the time and place of a final exam. Although it usually will be announced in class before exam time, knowledge of where and when the exam will be held is the student's responsibility.

8. Going to a test prepared also implies bringing along the right materials. This generally means having enough pens and pencils so that you won't have to run and sharpen pencils or search for a pen that works during the exam.

For some classes you will need to bring special paper, such as graph paper or theme paper. Have it on hand well before the exam day to save the panic of locating it at the last minute. It is a good idea for you to have a watch so that you need not rely on another student or the instructor to supply you with the time periodically throughout the test.

9. Keep contact with friends and classmates at a minimum during the last few minutes before an exam. Swapping questions before an exam can lead to heightened anxiety, especially if you are asked about or hear people talking about any aspect of the course content with which you are not absolutely confident. It can lead you to doubt yourself, your knowledge of the course content, or your ability to perform well on the test. Test panic can be contagious, and it is one disease you can do without.

DURING THE TEST

Whether you are taking an objective or subjective exam, approaching the task in an organized way is helpful, both for efficiency in the actual test-taking and reduction of anxiety.

ESSAY TESTS

One of the most important aspects of taking essay tests is the key or instructional words—those terms in the question itself which give direction to your answer. Even though you may know the material, failure to read the instructional words can be the difference between passing and failing. Comparing when you were asked to contrast, or explaining when you were asked to describe can lead to a heavy loss of points. If you don't follow the direction words, it is like not answering the question at all.

The ten most common key or instructional words are:

1. *Discuss*—requires that you carefully look at the topic and write about it in as much detail as possible, providing a lot of information, pointing out the issues, and giving the pros and cons.

Example: Discuss the role of the student as a participant in his or her own education.

2. *Explain*—requires that you clarify by stating reasons, giving meanings, or illustrating how a process works.

Example: Explain the necessity for a student to recite as part of the study process.

3. *Relate*—requires that you show how two or more things are connected and narrate, recount, or tell the story of an event or idea.

Example: Relate the steps in taking an essay test, making sure to include an illustration from a hypothetical test situation.

4. *Describe*—requires that you give a picture in words so that the reader can "see" what you are saying.

Example: Describe the process of previewing a chapter in a text.

5. *Define*—requires that you give meanings or describe something exactly.

Example: Define the term "plagiarism."

6. *Compare*—requires that you show how two or more things are both alike and/or different, weighing the features of each that are parallel.

Example: Compare the process of writing a term paper to that of writing a theme.

7. *Contrast*—requires that you show how two or more things are unlike or different.

Example: Contrast the purposes behind taking notes by underlining and forming organizational tables.

8. *Enumerate or list*—requires that you give the major points asked for in a listing format.

Example: Enumerate the steps a student follows in preparing for an exam.

9. *Summarize*—requires that you present in brief form an account or summary of the issues being called for.
Example: Summarize the major issues discussed in the chapter on concentration.

10. *Criticize*—requires that you analyze the material being called for, providing the good and bad points.
Example: Criticize underlining as a technique for taking notes from a textbook.

Some less common key words you are liable to encounter are:

Interpret—requires that you provide a meaning for what is being asked.
Example: Interpret the concept of an "efficient learner."

Justify—requires that you give proof or reasons, making sure that your argument is convincing.
Example: Justify the necessity for recitation after reading.

Trace—requires that you show the progress or history of what is being asked for.
Example: Trace the development of the ideas behind a student's thinking that math is an impossible subject to learn.

Prove—requires that you provide a logical argument and/or factual evidence to support the topic in order to prove that something is true or false.
Example: Provide a logical argument to support or refute the statement "Time-scheduling is the most important thing a student must learn to do."

GUIDELINES FOR TAKING ESSAY EXAMS

Step 1: Look Over the Test

As soon as you receive the test, quickly look at all the questions. Check to see whether you correctly anticipated any or all the questions during your exam preparation. Discovering that your crystal ball is in good working order is both an ego booster and an anxiety reducer.

Next to each question, jot down some key points that come to mind as you read it. This will ensure that you will have something to say for each question when you return to answer it later on in the test. As you read each question, notice the key words and how many parts the question contains. This will force you to put the question into your own words, helping you to understand what is being called for in the way of an answer.

Also notice the number of questions, their point value, and how much time you have to complete the test.

For example, questions with equal point values require equal time. A one-hour test consisting of five short essays, each worth twenty points, would mean allowing ten minutes for each question, or fifty minutes of the hour, leaving ten minutes for reviewing and revising the answers.

A one-hour test consisting of one long essay worth fifty points, one medium-length essay worth twenty points, and three short essays worth ten points apiece would be apportioned very differently. Since the three small essays are worth more than the twenty-pointer, it would mean giving them five minutes apiece, for a total of fifteen minutes, ten minutes to the twenty-pointer, and twenty-five to thirty minutes to the fifty-pointer. That still leaves five to ten minutes to review and revise.

It is especially important to distribute your time carefully on an essay test so that no question goes unanswered. You receive points for what is there, not for what you knew but did not get the time to put down on paper.

Step 2: Outline Your Answer

This is a brief but important process. As you begin to answer each question, recall what was asked and the number of parts to each question. Either mentally or on the side of the test or on a scrap of paper, briefly state what will be in each paragraph of your essay. Look at the following test question.

> High school and college math are quite different. Contrast some of the differences to a student just beginning a college math course. Also advise the student as to how to handle notes during a math lecture and what should be done to solve problems.

After you initially read the question, several ideas come to mind that can be put in the margin next to the question.

1. College math is done on your own.

2. Take notes on main ideas only.

3. Keep notes to a minimum.

4. Go over notes every day.

5. Solve problems by analyzing the problem first and then doing the math part.

When you go back to outline the question, it is apparent that there are three parts to the essay, which will mean a paragraph on the differences (contrasts) between high school and college math, a paragraph on note-taking during a math lecture, and a paragraph on problem-solving techniques.

Why bother going through all of this? There are several good reasons. First of all, it makes for a clear, well-organized essay. Any essay reader will tell you that a piece of written work that organizes the facts and presents them briefly and clearly is a clear winner over a piece of written work that contains all the facts but is disorganized and overly long. Second, by jotting down thoughts and outlining, you tend not to repeat the same facts in each essay. Since one fact cannot be more correct in one essay than in another, you run the risk of losing points by repetition where it is not appropriate. Third, by jotting down ideas and outlining, you ensure that you have something to say in each essay, thereby avoiding exam panic. Watching everyone else in the room write while you sit there and try to marshal your thoughts can cause you to lose valuable time in an essay test.

Step 3. Write Your Answer

The two steps listed above should take no more than three to five minutes. Now you are ready to write the answer. Begin with an introductory sentence that basically rewords the question and tells the readers what you are to say and what they will be reading. Follow your outline, or the parts of the question, and provide a paragraph for each part. Tie the whole bundle up with a concluding statement that sums up your answer, telling the readers what you have said and what they have just read.

Some further tips on writing an essay answer are:

- Stick to the subject. Don't pad your answer by giving the reader a lot of information not relevant to the question. This also implies not repeating yourself or your ideas.

- Use the elements of good writing you learned in English to construct a well-organized essay with complete sentences. For example, if you have several points to make, do it by saying: "First of all . . . in the second place . . . last of all," etc.

- Use qualifying statements rather than wrong facts. For example, if you are not sure of a particular date, qualify your answer. If you are not sure it was 1915 or 1925, write "within the first twenty years of this century." No one is suggesting that you won't be downgraded some points for not giving the exact date, but it probably will result in less of a loss of points than if you gave the wrong date.

- Write neatly. Legibility, as well as organization, is a strong influencing factor on a reader in grading an essay. If your writing becomes chicken tracks under pressure, consciously try to be neat. Print the test answers if need be, or write on every other line so that the reader can see the answer more clearly.

Step 4: Proofread Your Paper

Planning your time well means that you will have time to go back over and reread all the answers before turning in the test. At this time you want to:

- Check for misspelled words

- Check to see whether you have answered all the parts of the questions

- Check for grammatical errors

- Check for incorrectly stated facts, details, dates, etc.

GUIDELINES FOR TAKING OBJECTIVE EXAMS

Step 1: Look Over the Test

Just as in an essay test situation, your first task in taking an objective test is to look it over. You will want to notice the directions, the point distribution, the kinds of questions, and how many there are and then relate it all to the time available to complete the test.

In an essay test, the directions tend to be the key or instructional words within the structure of the question. In an objective test, the directions can also be within the body of a question; i.e., "Select the one answer that is the least correct." However, directions can appear at the beginning of the test or at the beginning of each new set of items. In other words, directions appear more frequently and in a greater variety of places on an objective test than on an essay test.

As you look over the test, notice the point distribution. Most frequently, all questions on an objective test are worth the same number of points. Sometimes, however, certain sections of a test are worth more per question than others. If all are worth the same number of points, say two or three points apiece, you will want to distribute your time equally over all the items. If one section or set of questions is worth more, you will want to spend more time on those in order to receive the maximum number of points possible in relation to your knowledge of the material or the difficulty of the items.

As you look at the questions, notice the kinds of objective questions you are being asked to answer. The various kinds include:

MULTIPLE-CHOICE ITEMS

These are the most frequently used type of objective question. Basically they are nothing more than a sophisticated true-false question. There is a stem plus several alternative answers. By reading the stem and each alternative and determining whether it is true or false, you will be able to figure out the best answer. Look at the following multiple-choice question:

> The group with the highest incidence of reported cases of venereal disease is
> a. under 25 years of age
> b. under 15 years of age
> c. over 30 years of age
> d. over 25 years of age

Read the stem and each one of the alternative answers like this:

- The group with the highest incidence of reported cases of venereal disease is under 25 years of age.

- The group with the highest incidence of reported cases of venereal disease is under 15 years of age.

- The group with the highest incidence of reported cases of venereal disease is over 30 years of age.

- The group with the highest incidence of reported cases of venereal disease is over 25 years of age.

As you read each one, determine whether it is true or false. The one to which you can apply the true answer is the correct one. The right answer is (a), by the way.

MATCHING ITEMS

Matching questions contain two sets of facts or statements that are related to each other in some way. For example, one list may be the names of several authors; the other, the names of books they have written. Your job would be to match the author with the proper book title.

1. Charles Dickens	A. *Huckleberry Finn*
2. Mark Twain	B. *The Scarlet Letter*
3. Ernest Hemingway	C. *A Tale of Two Cities*
4. John Irving	D. *For Whom the Bell Tolls*
5. Nathaniel Hawthorne	E. *The World According to Garp*

Begin by going through the first list and identifying all those items which you can match up with their counterparts in the second list. Then go back and work through the remaining items which you are less sure of or do not know the answer to at all. You will have to use strategies such as elimination or similarity between the items in the two columns to divine some of the answers. The right answers to the question above are 1 (c), 2 (a), 3 (d), 4 (e), and 5 (b).

There are a variety of combinations that can be presented for pairing up: vocabulary words matched with their definitions or functions, dates matched with the events they represent, or events matched with their significance. Major parts may be matched with their components, such as heart paired with valves and aorta, or a component may be matched with its whole, such as heart matched with the circulatory system, or development section matched with the term "symphony."

TRUE-FALSE ITEMS

True-false items are statements presented for the test-taker to read and make a determination as to their being true (correct) or false (not correct). It is wrong, however, to think that true-false items deal only with facts. They can be concerned with the statistics, ideas, concepts, or definitions in a course or can be statements about applications of a principle or summaries of information relating to course material.

True-false items call for a thorough knowledge of the subject material since there are few hints to be gathered from the other items in the test to help you determine the answer.

There are, however, some clue words which are associated with the potential rightness or wrongness of an answer. Some words help in pointing the way to a false answer, others to a true answer.

False implies that the answer is absolute—it can be one way and one way only. Therefore, any words appearing in the test items associated with being absolute, or allowing for no exception, usually indicate that the statement is false. Some of these words are:

always	never	must
none	all	impossible
only	merely	necessarily
absolutely	completely	

There are words appearing in true-false items that are associated with the correctness or truth of an item. These are not absolute words, and they allow for variation or exception. They usually indicate that the statement is true. Some of these words are:

seldom	often	generally
may	perhaps	usually
sometimes	frequently	

Read these items and try to determine whether they are true or false:

__1. Constructing a time schedule always leads to improved grades.

__2. The average age of college freshmen seems to be getting higher each year.

__3. Tests are used by instructors to accurately measure a student's ability.

__4. Making flash cards is one way to study a foreign language.

__5. Concentration is impossible if a student studies in a noisy environment.

__6. Previewing a chapter generally results in a faster reading rate.

__7. Instructors often use exams to measure what a student learned in a course.

__8. In order to learn vocabulary, it is necessary for a student to make vocabulary flash cards.

Statements 1, 3, 5, and 8 are false. What words in each item led you to select that answer?

_____ _____ _____ _____

Statements 2, 4, 6, and 7 are true. What words in each item led you to select that answer?

_____ _____ _____ _____

FILL-IN-THE-BLANKS ITEMS
Fill-in-the-blanks test items are phrases, sentences, or even whole paragraphs with blank spaces left for the insertion of significant words that show you understand how to complete the statement accurately.

Finally, you will want to relate all this information to the time you have in which to do the test. The time you spend on each item will depend on the points given for each item, the number of items on the test, and the difficulty of the test.

For example, fifty true-false or multiple-choice items that are worth 2 points each in a test lasting seventy-five minutes means you will have to work quickly and accurately, moving through the test, answering the questions you know, giving yourself time to return to the unknown items, and leaving time for a quick scan of the entire test before you turn it in.

However, in a test consisting of matching, multiple-choice, and true-false items, where one set of items is worth at least half the number of points on the entire test and the other two sets of questions are worth half the remaining points apiece, you must use a different time strategy. You will have to give the most heavily weighted set of items about half the entire test time and the other two sets one-quarter of the test time each.

Even if you are prepared for a test, failure to look it over carefully, plan your test-taking strategy well, and stick to your schedule can cause you to come out with a grade that does not reflect your ability or knowledge of the course content.

Step 2: Answer the Question

Keeping your plan in mind, proceed to answer the questions.

It is important, especially in a multiple-choice test, to read the stem of the question and all the possible answers. In their haste to get through a test, or because of carelessness, many students read through the alternatives till they come to an answer they feel is correct, even if they have not read all the choices, mark the answer, and go on. This can be costly. Look at the following example:

Animals in the feline family include
  a. elephants
  b. cats
  c. tigers
  d. two of the above

A hasty reading could mean that you mark (b) as the answer and skip to the next question. Because you marked the first known right answer without having read all the alternatives, you would receive no credit for the item in a test situation.

Answer the easiest items first. Go through the test and do all the questions you know. If you cannot decide between two answers, put a dot beside the two choices and keep moving through the test. For those you do not know at all, skip over them.

Step 3: Go Over the Test Again

Having gone through the test once, go through again and do the items you checked as "unsure" on the first go-round.

Finally, do the items for which you do not know the answers. In other words, guess. Research indicates that as long as there is no penalty for guessing on a test, it is to your advantage to go ahead and make a stab at an answer, even if you are unsure of it. In most classroom tests there is usually no penalty for guessing. In some standardized tests there is. In that case, you will want to guess with care, making sure you can eliminate some of the choices before guessing so as to raise your odds of coming up with the right answer. It is always safe to ask whether there is a penalty for guessing when taking a standardized test—those tests not made by an instructor which come printed up and frequently are requirements for entrance into programs or schools or are tests of aptitude or intelligence.

Similarly, research indicates that you should feel free to change your answer if you change your mind. Chances are, evidence found elsewhere in the test will lead you to rethink an answer. At any rate, the odds are in your favor. Besides, it is only a myth that the first impression is the right one.

TESTWISENESS

If you prepare well and follow all the hints for taking a test, you probably feel you are wise enough. What is testwiseness?

Testwiseness refers to clues or hints within the multiple-choice test items themselves that can help you locate the answer when your study techniques fail and you cannot recognize the answer from among the choices. Being testwise assists you in eliminating answers, a process that raises the odds of determining the correct answer when you need to guess. From an in-depth study of a large variety of exam questions, it has been determined that the alternatives frequently contain clues to the answer.

Being testwise is *no substitute for proper test preparation*. It is one more tool or technique to aid you in being as good a student as you can possibly be.

If your instructor is a good test-maker, it probably will not work well. If you haven't studied adequately, it probably will not be an effective tool. Nothing replaces effective study. If you use these clues as a tool when all else fails, you can eliminate some alternatives and then be able to focus on the remaining choices.

The following testwiseness clues will help in selecting the correct alternatives if you are not sure of an answer. Although you should take advantage of these clues when you need to, I repeat, it is not wise to depend on them.

Length Clue
Frequently, the clue to the correct answer lies in the length of the answers given, with one being significantly longer (or shorter) than the others. For example:

To increase the effectiveness of communications, a person should
    a. speak louder
    b. use language that is clear, concise, and appropriate
    c. take a course
    d. increase their vocabulary

Most General Clue

Frequently, the correct answer is the most general one, the one that allows for variation. It is a situation much like the one described earlier in the section on true-false items. When you examine the stem and each alternative, the one that is true, or most general, is correct. The other alternatives are generally more technical, allow for no variation, and are, therefore, false. For example:

Dinosaurs are called the "ruling reptiles" because they
    a. were 82 feet tall
    b. had birdlike hips
    c. developed spectacularly during the Mesozoic Period
    d. were carnivores

Item (c) is the most correct and most general answer, allowing for variation. Some dinosaurs were as small as chickens, some had reptilelike hips, and some were herbivores. Therefore, (a), (b), and (d) are untrue.

Middle Value Clue

Frequently, the alternatives in an answer are a set of four or five numbers, such as dates or statistics. If you are not sure of the correct answer, eliminate the highest and lowest numbers and select from remaining answers. For example:

Sigmund Freud was born in
    a. 1832
    b. 1856
    c. 1901
    d. 1947

If you eliminate the extremes, 1832 and 1947, which are too early and too late, respectively, your choices are narrowed to 1856 and 1901. The correct answer is 1856.

Two Alike Clue

Sometimes two of the alternatives, although worded differently, basically mean the same thing. Since neither can be more correct than the other, eliminate any two items that mean the same thing. For example:

The purpose of a résumé is to
  a. document your work experience
  b. supply the potential employer with a list of references
  c. sell yourself to an employer
  d. list all the jobs you have had

Since alternatives (a) and (d) are basically the same, you should eliminate them and select your answer from the remaining two alternatives. The correct answer is (c).

Two Opposites Clue

Sometimes two of the alternatives have opposite meanings. The correct answer probably is in that pair. Eliminate the other choices and pick from the pair of opposites. For example:

After vein surgery, the following nursing actions should be carried out:
  a. keep patient's leg elevated while in bed
  b. keep the dressing moist
  c. have the patient dangle his or her feet three times daily
  d. wrap the legs in elastic bandages

Alternatives (a) and (c) are opposites. By eliminating the other two choices, you then select the answer from the pair of opposites. The correct answer is (a).

Those Known to Be Correct Clue

Some multiple-choice questions are made up of a statement and a series of possible answers followed by a series of choices. You are usually asked to select answers based on how many from the list of choices are correct—either one, two, three, all of the above, or none of the above. The choice is made either from numbers or from a series of statements—two of the above, one of the above, none of the above, etc.

The best way to handle this type of question is to read each stem and alternative and determine whether it is true or false. Once you have found a true statement, the choice "none of the above" is no longer viable. Similarly, once you have found a false statement, the choice "all of the above" is no longer viable. The remaining answers, "one of the above," etc., no longer apply.

Frequently, you know that the stem and one or two of the alternatives are true. However, the possible answers include choices which you are unsure of. In that case, you would have to select the answer that contains an unknown to you. For example:

Which of the following are true statements related to the treatment of chemically dependent persons?
1. Antabuse reduces impulse drinking.
2. Methadone allows the patient to continue his or her habit in a more acceptable way.
3. AA is primarily for patients who have not been in a treatment center.
4. Live-in treatment centers are the only way to arrest the disease.
   a. three of the above
   b. two of the above
   c. one of the above
   d. none of the above
   e. all of the above

Looking at the alternatives, you recognize statement 4 as being false; the specific word "only" makes it a statement without exception. Therefore, answer (e) is not a viable option. You know that statement 3 is also not true because most people in AA have gone through some form of treatment prior to their membership. Therefore, (a) is not a choice, and (b), (c), and (d) remain. When you discover that statement 2 is true, (d) is no longer a potential answer. Answers (b) and (c) remain. If you know that statement 1 is also true, you realize that the correct answer is (b).

You also may be asked to select an answer for this type of question when the choices are written out in this fashion:

   a. 1, 2
   b. 1, 3
   c. 2, 3, and 4
   d. 2, 4

Since you know 2 is a true statement, you have to pick from answers (a), (c), and (d). When you eliminate statements 3 and 4, (b), (c), and (d) drop out, leaving (a), which contains a known and an unknown. Answer (a) is the correct answer.

These are difficult test questions that demand a good command of the material. If you need to guess, work with those items which you know to be correct and stick with the unknowns that go with them.

Word Association Clue

Another way to recognize an answer is to look for clues in the choices that relate to the stem of the item. For example:

   A Tale of Two Cities is about:
   a. the Hardy boys
   b. the American Revolution

    c. a fabled island
    d. London and Paris

Even if you know nothing about the contents or author of the book, the fact that it is about two cities is clue enough so that you make the association between the title and alternative (d).

Here are a few multiple-choice items from actual classroom tests. Read each test question and determine what testwiseness clue you would use to help locate the answer.

1. Sinus tachycardia is considered to be present when the heart is beating faster than:
    a. 85 beats per minute
    b. 60 beats per minute
    c. 120 beats per minute
    d. 100 beats per minute

CLUE: _____

2. Which of the following anatomical structures prevents blood from leaving the right ventricle and entering the right atrium?
    a. bicuspid valve
    b. pulmonary valve
    c. semilunar valve
    d. tricuspid valve

CLUE: _____

3. Good communications should be:
    a. immediate
    b. spontaneous
    c. concerned with the here and now
    d. a and b
    e. b and c
    f. a and c
    g. all of the above
    h. none of the above

CLUE: _____

4. Which of the following is a proper nursing action after a gastrointestinal examination?
    a. administer milk of magnesia
    b. watch for signs of gastrointestinal irritation
    c. administer antacids to reduce gastric acidity
    d. return the patient to his or her room

CLUE: _____

5. The power of the President is derived from:
    a. his or her image

b. his or her powers of persuasion
c. a combination of constitutional authority, past precedent, and legislative enactment
d. his or her intelligence

CLUE: _____
6. Personality disorders:
   a. are a direct result of medical problems
   b. are a diverse group of disorders with a common pattern of deviant behavior
   c. result in a great deal of stress to the individual
   d. are genetically transmitted

CLUE: _____
7. The rods and cones of the visual system:
   a. are axons which carry information to the brain
   b. are receptors for light energy which starts the process of generating new impulses
   c. are ganglion cells
   d. carry sound waves to the cochlea

CLUE: _____

The Answers:

Item	Clue	Correct Answer
1.	Middle value clue	d
2.	Two opposites clue (a and d)	d
3.	Those known to be correct clue	g
4.	Two alike clue (a and c)	b
5.	Length clue	c
6.	Most general clue	b
7.	Word association clue	b

EXAM PANIC

Tests make everyone a bit anxious, and that is quite normal. We all need that extra bit of adrenalin to facilitate the completion of unpleasant tasks. It is when that extra juice gets out of hand, heightening physiological responses, that it becomes debilitating and exam panic sets in. Maybe you have had it happen. You believe you have prepared well for a test. You arrive in plenty of time, read and recognize the questions and their potential answers, and set out to write the test. Then you go blank. When the test is over, you walk out of the room and remember the answers. That is exam panic. It is a heightened physiological response—pupil dilation, sweaty palms, increased blood pressure, butterflies in the stomach, and perhaps a knot in the neck, back, or other part of the body. No need to tell you if you have known it.

Some students become anxious before the exam, any time from the moment the test is announced through the study or preparation time. Tests cause them to become irritable, which in turn produces poor concentration and reduced efficiency at tasks, especially studying. For some it results in feeling more tired than usual, headaches, and/or poor sleeping patterns, perhaps including insomnia.

Why does it happen? First of all, it can occur if you are not well prepared and know it. You sit there looking at the test questions and are unable to come up with the answers. As the minutes go by, you get more nervous, increasing your body responses and decreasing your ability to think and answer the questions.

Some students experience exam panic even though they are well-prepared. This happens because the exam may represent a large obstacle to be cleared in order to achieve something else. For example, students hoping to enter nursing, dental, or veterinary programs frequently experience exam panic in science courses which represent prerequisites for entrance into the program and the future they want. Unless they do well in the science courses, a lot of preparation, decision making, and even hopes and dreams can go down the tube. This syndrome occurs in other similar situations, too, such as entrance tests, IQ tests, etc.

Students on scholarship may become anxious, because in order to maintain their financial aid, they realize that they must do well. The exam may represent the difference between maintaining a scholarship or losing it, and ultimately between an education and no education.

Students who have not been in school for a while may see an exam as the prediction of or answer to the question of their ability to be a student. If the image they have of themselves as a student is a poor one (based on information from previous schooling), even adequate preparation is not enough to calm jittery nerves. Frequently, this image was suggested by someone else, and when the student panics on the exam and consequently does not do well, the image is fulfilled. Unfortunately, the thinking process surrounding exam panic becomes circular and hard to break with each new exam experience.

No matter what the reason, test anxiety involves negative internal messages—things you say to yourself that probably help trigger the reaction. Is this familiar?

This vicious circle occurs frequently. It has as many variations as there are students who suffer test panic. It is possible to overcome test panic.

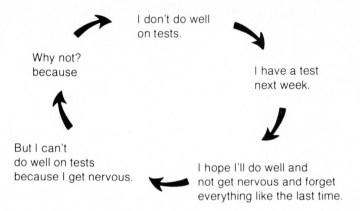

I don't do well on tests.

Why not? because

I have a test next week.

But I can't do well on tests because I get nervous.

I hope I'll do well and not get nervous and forget everything like the last time.

WHAT TO DO

1. Always prepare thoroughly for a test and use good strategies during the actual taking of the test to help inhibit anxiety responses.

2. Examine your anxiety responses when they occur.

   Complete the following self-examination quiz:

	OCCASIONALLY	FAIRLY OFTEN	ALWAYS
I tend to get anxious			
—when a test is announced			
—while preparing for a test			
—as the time for the test draws closer			
—while taking the test			
—after the test is over			
—when it is a surprise test			
For me, test panic means			
—a rapid heartbeat			
—sweaty palms			
—a sick stomach			
—tenseness in my body			
—excessive perspiration			
—headache			

Now look at the results of your self-examination and complete the following statements by writing a few sentences describing yourself in relation to the situation(s) that cause you the most anxiety and the worst physiological responses.

I tend to get anxious _____

_____

_____

My body reacts by _____

_____

Now look at your responses again, this time in relation to the kind and degree of anxiety and your ability to manage it.

	LITTLE OR NO ANXIETY	SOME ANXIETY	A LOT OF ANXIETY BUT MANAGEABLE	BEYOND MY CONTROL
When a test is announced				
While preparing for a test				
As the time for a test draws closer				
While taking a test				
After the test is over				
When it is a surprise test				

Remember, it was stated that anxiety is basically a matter of heightened physiology as well as a usual response to a situation—panic during some phase of the testing process. To overcome test panic, it is necessary to decrease the physiology causing the anxiety and to learn a new response, a relaxation response, to a tension-producing situation, namely, the testing process. To reduce anxiety, then, it is necessary to learn relaxation techniques. Read through the following relaxation exercise, or better yet, have someone else read it to you while you do the drill. Then you can do the same for a classmate. Still another possibility is to tape-record the exercise, making it a more permanent record.

Relaxation Exercise

Learning to relax will help you reduce tension, nervousness, and anxiety. It is simply not possible to be very anxious, tense, or nervous when your body is completely relaxed.

Try to get as relaxed as possible in a short time. As you practice relaxing, you will find that you will become better and better at it and will be able to develop a relaxed state very quickly. This exercise is meant to give you practice until you can relax quickly and easily without any instructions.

Sit back in a chair and get as comfortable as possible. Before you begin to relax, notice all the little pressures and tensions in your body.

Check your feet and legs. Do they feel completely loose and relaxed? Now your head. Are there strains in your neck muscles or jaws?

Close your eyes and try to relax all the tension you found. Breathe normally and concentrate on feeling heavy all over. You should feel more calm and relaxed than you did a few minutes ago.

Now work up to a deeper level of relaxation. You will have to locate the tensions and systematically remove them. First, try to tense every muscle in your body, from your head to your toes—jaws tight, neck tight and stiff, forehead wrinkled and tense, arms and hands tense, fists clenched, stomach and chest muscles tight, legs and feet tensed. You should now be tense all over. Hold that tension for another moment and then let go all over. Breathe normally and feel the wave of relaxation spread through your body. You may feel a kind of warm glow or slightly tingling sensation as the relaxation flows in. Relax as completely as possible. Concentrate on feeling heavy in your chair. Notice the lack of tension everywhere in your body.

Now find all the remaining tensions in your body and remove them. Keep the rest of your body as relaxed as before, but tighten up your toes and your foot muscles. Notice the tension in your toes, the tops of your feet, and the sides of your ankles. Now relax your feet completely. Notice the contrast. Now tense the same muscles again—hold it now, relax. Feel the relaxation. Note the heaviness in your feet. Now keep all the rest of your body relaxed while you tense your leg and thigh muscles. Feel your legs rise a little as your thigh muscles lighten. The backs of your legs should be hard and tight. Hold that tension for a moment and then relax. Notice the heaviness in your legs and thighs. Your whole body should be limp and at rest in the chair.

Tighten your stomach muscles. Notice that you feel like you do when you are anxious or angry or in a tense or dangerous situation. Hold the tension for a moment and then relax. Repeat that again. Tense the stomach muscles, hold it, and then relax.

Do the same with your chest muscles. Notice that when you tense your chest muscles, the tension goes up into your shoulders and upper arms. Hold it for a minute and then relax. Again, tense and relax. Again, tense. And relax. You should now be relaxed all over. Check to be sure that the rest of your body is relaxed and loose.

Clench your right fist and tense your arm muscles—forearm and biceps. Hold the tension in the right hand and arm and tense the left fist and arm. Tighten both more.Study the tension. Locate it in each arm. Hold it. Now relax. Straighten out your fingers and let the comfortable, loose, restful feeling flow into your arms, hands, and the rest of your body. One more time. Tense both hands and arms and hold it. Now let go and relax.

Tighten your face and neck muscles. Close your eyes, wrinkle your forehead, and tighten your jaws with your teeth together. Hold it for a moment and then relax. Try it again with all the same muscles tight—jaws tight, neck muscles tense all the way down into the back. Relax. Notice all the changes as you relax. Your forehead and scalp smooth out, your lips and jaws relax, your mouth is open a little, and your shoulders are loose and free to move.

You have now relaxed all the major areas of your body, and you should be relaxed all over. Try to go over all the areas and make sure there are no tensions left in your feet and legs or your thighs. Stomach and chest are relaxed.

Relax your chest, shoulders, arms, and hands. Relax all the neck muscles, the jaws, and face, and the scalp muscles. Keep relaxing your whole body. It feels loose, heavy, calm, quiet, and at rest.

Increase the relaxation by taking a really deep breath and exhaling slowly. Close your eyes and notice how you become less aware of anything but your own hushed, mellow, comfort. You feel like soft velvet—tranquil, peaceful, and serene. You blend into the chair. You feel placid and gentle, unwilling to move a muscle. Just raising your arm would be an effort. Even thinking about it is an effort. Drop back into comfort; relax the slight tensions in your arm from thinking about moving it.

Now you are all quiet and relaxed. You can observe the lack of tension all through your body. Now try to become more relaxed. Try to become more relaxed each time you breathe out. Notice the deeper and deeper relaxation as you become more calm and serene.

You can go relaxing in this way for as long as you wish. When you are ready to get up, simply count backwards—5, 4, 3, 2, 1—open your eyes, and notice that you are refreshed, calm, and wide awake. You feel fine.

Suggestions for Use of Relaxation Techniques

Once you have learned the relaxation routine, you can use it before a study session. Before beginning to study for a test, sit in a comfortable chair and go through the relaxation drill. Once you are feeling comfortable, proceed to your desk. During the study session, stop if you feel tension or anxiety creeping into your body. Turn away from the books and relax. Work on the areas of tension until your body feels calm again.

You can, of course, also use the relaxation drill before an exam or during it. When you sit down to take the exam, quickly relax your body. If during the exam you are sidetracked by tension, take a few seconds and use relaxation as a first-aid measure. In this situation, you can relax only those areas in which you are tense, such as your neck, shoulders, or back. Take a deep breath, hold it for ten to fifteen seconds, and slowly let it out. It is both a mind-clearer and a body-relaxer.

Here is something else to practice. When you are relaxing in a chair before studying, try to form a mental picture of yourself sitting in a chair in a classroom and taking a test. Take a mental and physical measurement of your body's tension when you see this scene. Relax those areas which feel tense when you see and think about yourself in the test situation. See yourself again in the classroom. Take a new measurement and do some more relaxation. Continue to alternate these two items, relaxation and visualization of yourself in the test situation, until the measurement of yourself in the testing scene registers "comfortable."

Many schools have math/test anxiety programs or members of the advising or counseling staff who can help further with the problem if these self-help measures prove inadequate to your particular situation.

AFTER THE EXAM

If hindsight were perfect vision, students would ace every exam. Since that tends not to be the case, at least use the experience and knowledge gained from taking an exam toward the preparation for and taking of the next one.

Most instructors are fairly consistent, and the first exam in a course should serve as a model for future tests.

When you get the test back, go over it carefully, noting such things as:

• The types of questions on the test

• The depth of knowledge required for the test

• The kinds of questions you got wrong or right

Good decisions are based on accurate information. Making choices as to what and how you will study for the next exam will be helped immeasurably by the information you gather about the test and your performance on the previous one.

SUMMARY

—Exams are not unusual punishment but a good way of evaluating yourself in relation to the course. The more frequent the exams, the better it is for the student.

—Take an exam, either objective or subjective, systematically. Read the directions, skim the test, make a schedule based on the number of questions and their point value in relation to the time available, and always leave time to go back over the test to correct errors or complete questions.

—If all else fails, use testwiseness clues as an emergency aid to guessing in an objective test when you truly do not know the answer.
—If you experience exam panic, try to figure out its roots and work to alleviate it, either by yourself or with the help of a trained person.
—Always use exam results, good or bad, to prepare for and take the next test.

WRITING PAPERS IN COLLEGE | 8

This chapter is concerned with college writing assignments—term papers and themes in particular. Each of the two main sections deals with

- What term papers and themes are

- Why they are assigned

- The kinds of term papers and themes that are assigned

- The time factor in the preparation of papers and themes

- The steps to follow in writing papers and themes

- Further suggestions regarding grammar, style, etc.

Mentally review your experiences in writing term papers and themes, and then write down your thoughts. My experiences in writing papers and

themes has been _____

_____

_____

_____

_____

Therefore, based on your self-evaluation, the things you will want to pay particular attention to in this chapter are:

_____

_____

_____

_____

There are two basic types of writing you will do in college. One involves research and data from other sources, and the other involves a more personal expression of ideas from your own experience. Term papers are usually assigned in courses with data-based knowledge, such as psychology, history, sociology, or marketing. Themes are usually assigned in courses designed to teach you how to write. In either case, a well-planned, systematic approach to the assignment will help get the job done with minimum anguish and maximum effectiveness.

TERM PAPERS

Many students have never written a term paper before they are confronted with the task in a college course. The aspects of the assignment that scare them the most are how to select a subject and how to locate information in the library. Both problems will be dealt with, the first in this chapter and the second in Chapter 9.

No matter what your concern or level of expertise in writing term papers, they are an established fact of college life. Doing research is like doing a puzzle. You select pieces from many sources, and you get to see the picture when it all fits together. It is actually one of the most exciting college assignments you can get. Many college instructors get very discouraged when they read the results of students' efforts at writing term papers, because of the students' failure to see the task as a challenge and a chance to display individual effort and creativity.

Term papers are a recorded summary of extensive reading on a topic freely chosen or instructor-selected, done by students from sources outside the assigned class reading.

Simply stated, a good term paper is an organized effort on your part to search out and present relevant information on a topic in such a way that the reader gets an overall picture of the subject matter. Term papers are assigned because the instructor wants you to go beyond the scope of the classroom coverage of a topic and look into it in more depth.

In introductory courses, a term paper can represent going beyond the basics in one area so that you can get a better feeling for some aspects of a subject covered briefly in class. For example, religious belief systems are usually discussed in Cultural Anthropology 101. The instructor requires a term paper on an in-depth study of a religious belief system in one particular culture to allow students to see and report on the many ways in which the system influences a people.

In a more advanced course, a term paper can represent a going beyond the basics to include not only reading of outside sources but an integration of that knowledge with new material, Here the instructor assumes more than a mere reporting of what is read, a putting together of old and new information, and the drawing of conclusions or the stating of new ideas.

In the third course in cultural anthropology, the instructor may require a term paper dealing with religious belief systems across cultures. This assumes comparisons, contrasts, and conclusions you can draw about religious belief systems and how they operate in different groups.

These examples represent the types of term papers assigned, with one being a nonevaluative, straight reporting of information on a topic from a variety of sources and the other two representing a reporting of information plus evaluative comments on a topic, also from a variety of sources. The material to be reported on can represent ideas (the concept of behavioral engineering), facts (the history of behavioral engineering), people (B. F. Skinner, father of behavioral engineering), or a combination of these aspects (B. F. Skinner and the concept of behavioral engineering: an ethical consideration).

THE TIME FACTOR IN WRITING A TERM PAPER

Term papers are usually assigned six to ten weeks before they are due. Most instructors are familiar with the amount of time and energy required to produce a good paper; thus the liberal time allowance. Most students, however, put off writing a paper and thereby let the time advantage slip away. Paper-writing is no different from any other piece of deadline work. It needs to be spaced out over time for you to do the best job possible, ensure comprehension and integration of all the material read for the paper, and write coherently and thoughtfully. A paper crammed into three or five days is no different from a quarter's worth of content material crammed into three or five days of studying. It becomes jumbled and incoherent. Cramming for a paper, like cramming for a test, usually means that all other work is stopped; when the project is finished, a fast game of catch up is required. Since most papers are due at the end of a term, the work put off is usually test preparation.

In the next section, steps for writing a paper will be presented. First, let's fit those steps into a time frame. The first plan will be for a paper with a six-week time limit, the second for a paper with a ten-week limit. As is the case with other work, well-planned, well-spaced assignments get done with a minimum of anxiety, allowing time for all the activities that are necessary in your life as a student, worker, family member, etc. Note that the actual work is fitted into five and nine weeks, respectively. Giving yourself a mental deadline earlier than the actual one allows for any contingencies that might throw your schedule off course. Since a student's life is rarely without a few minor traumas, you may as well plan your time to take the unexpected into account. Read Example 8.1.

EXAMPLE

8.1

Time frame for writing a term paper

STEPS IN WRITING A TERM PAPER	TIME FRAME	
	5 WEEKS	9 WEEKS
1. Selecting a subject	2 days	4 days
2. Selecting reading materials	5 days	10 days
3. Making notes from reading materials	10 days	2 weeks
4. Giving direction to the paper: the outline	4 days	1 week
5. Writing the first draft	10 days	2 weeks
6. Editing the paper	2 days	1 week
7. Typing the paper	2 days	1 week

With either schedule, you still have one week remaining before the actual due date to either sit back and gloat over your accomplishment or complete the term paper.

STEPS IN WRITING A TERM PAPER

Step 1: Selecting a Subject

Most students consider selecting a subject the most difficult aspect of paper-writing. Indeed, it is an area that gives a lot of trouble, and it is probably the most crucial step in the process. Since the subject defines the scope of the paper, selection of a suitable subject is all-important. Sometimes the instructor sets the theme of the paper, either in a general or a specific way. A general assignment would be to write on some aspect of World War II, and a specific assignment would be to write on the new technology in weaponry in World War II that led to the age of space travel in the 1960s and 1970s.

Sometimes the choice of a topic is left entirely to the student. Most students tend to select a subject that is too broad to be handled in the amount of pages assigned. The average term paper is about ten pages. If you select a topic that has infinite possibilities, chances are your reading will be too varied, constructing an outline and thesis statement will be difficult, and your writing will be scattered and vague. Therefore, begin with a large idea and refine it till you have a topic you can handle in the number of pages assigned.

Where does the large idea come from? It usually comes from some exploratory reading from a source, such as a general encyclopedia article or another text dealing with the subject. In either case, you will get general ideas from which you can start to work to narrow the topic.

For example, let's assume you are in an art history class and have been assigned to write a paper on Pablo Picasso. By itself that is too large a subject to be handled in the required ten pages. You've seen a few of his paintings in class but know little about him. Therefore, you go to the encyclopedia, look up his name, and read about him. There you find a lengthy article describing his life, work, and ideas on art. You learn something about the evolution of his ideas on drawing the human figure, from a rather classical Greek interpretation of the body to a distortion of the human form with geometric shapes. You recall seeing a few of these paintings and wondering why they were painted in that manner. Now you have an idea. Suppose, you say to yourself, you write on the evolution of the human figure in the works of Pablo Picasso, delineating his ideas and supporting them by quotes from his writings and by examples from selected paintings depicting the two types of forms. You have narrowed down the subject to one aspect of a very complicated topic that can be handled in the space assigned. You read about the subject broadly, found an aspect that interested you, and then designated a focus for that interest. You could say that your paper was going to reflect an answer to the question, What were Picasso's evolutionary ideas on the drawing of the human figure, and in what works are examples found?

Let's take another example. Suppose you were asked to write a paper on efficient study skills. Whole books have been written on the subject, and so it's necessary to narrow it down to a reasonable aspect of the topic, let's say five pages.

You might first narrow it to focus on the area of efficient study skills for textbook usage. You could then decide you want to focus on the note-taking aspect of text study skills. You could focus even more sharply by concentrating on note-taking study skills for coping with science textbooks.

Take the same topic and narrow down a subject for a five-page paper.

1. Topic "Efficient Study Skills" _____

2. Main focus area _____

3. Refined focus area _____

4. Final focus area _____

Now try another topic.

1. Topic "Selecting a Career" _____

2. Main focus area _____

3. Refined focus area _____

4. Final focus area _____

Additional Ways to Narrow a Subject

Basically then, refining a subject for a term paper involves preliminary reading and questioning to arrive at a suitable topic.

Here are some ways you can question the material in order to refine it. Assume you are in a nursing program and have been asked to write a paper on an aspect of nursing. From your exploratory reading, you decide to focus on pediatric nursing, because of your interest in children. You can then focus the subject by dealing with a specific aspect of pediatric nursing. You can limit the focus by dealing with:

A specific *kind* of pediatric nursing, e.g., pediatric nursing with terminally ill children.

A specific *aspect* of pediatric nursing, e.g., pediatric nurses as counselors to parents or pediatric nurses as communicators with children.

A specific *example* of pediatric nursing, e.g., pediatric nurses in Metropolitan General Hospital.

A specific *experience* in pediatric nursing, e.g., the training experiences of pediatric nurses.

A specific *time* period in the history of pediatric nursing, e.g., pediatric nursing in the 1970s.

A specific *person* in pediatric nursing, e.g., Ms. X, the pediatric nurse.

A specific *place* in pediatric nursing, e.g., pediatric nursing in Boston's Children's Hospital.

Working with a topic of your choice, limit your focus by using the same guidelines:

Topic: _____

A specific kind of _____

A specific aspect of _____

A specific example of _____

A specific experience in _____

A specific time _____

A specific person _____

A specific place _____

You can also focus your subject by thinking about the topic in terms of the questions you want your paper to answer. For example:

Define the subject by asking, What does it mean?

Describe the subject by asking, What does it look like?

Compare the subject by asking, How does it compare with (or how is it similar to) some other subject?

Contrast the subject by asking, How is it different from some other subject?

Classify the subject by asking, What are the different types of

_____?

Report on the subject by asking, What are the facts about

_____?

Interpret the subject by asking, What is the meaning behind

_____?

Reflect on the subject by asking, What are my (or other people's) responses to or observations on the subject?

Evaluate the subject by asking, What is the value or importance of

_____?

Argue about the subject by asking, What case(s) can be made for or

against _____?

What are the parts of _____?

Analyze the subject by asking, How is _____ made? How

does _____ function? What causes _____ to operate in this manner?

In summary, selection of a subject for a term paper involves carefully choosing and limiting a topic, regardless of whether the instructor or the student sets the limits.

Narrow the topic so that it satisfies you from the standpoint of interest and the possibility of finding sources of information. A boring subject will mean difficulty in sustaining interest and will probably result in an uninteresting paper. The topic must be manageable based on the depth of coverage expected. A five-page paper on agriculture is too broad, and the sources are too numerous. Five pages on spinach farming in Ohio would be too narrow, and the sources would be nonexistent. Farm implement innovations during the last three to five years would probably be about right for both the topic and the resources.

Step 2: Selecting Reading Materials

Selecting materials for a term paper means going to the library to find sources of information.

This section will assume you know how to use a library to find source material for a paper. If you do not have that familiarity, it is suggested that you work through Chapter 9 and then come back to this section.

Once you have selected a topic, you will have to prepare a bibliography—a compilation of books, magazines, or newspaper articles and possibly reference sources in which you will locate the information to be used for your paper.

The first step is to arm yourself with a large supply of 3 by 5 cards and go to the library. Head for the card catalog and look up the major subject heading of your paper. Once you find the topic heading, look through the books listed and make a bibliography card for each book you feel might contain potential information for the paper. Don't be worried about having too many books. Many that you look at won't contain the information you need, or if they do, it will not be presented as well or as completely as in another source.

Your bibliography cards for books will look like the one shown in Example 8.2.

After you have written down the sources for the main topic, search your mind for all the other possible headings under which you might locate information. For example, if your main heading is Business ethics, other possible topics under which you would look might be: Ethics, Business, Morals, _____

_____

Under most major categories there is a "see also" card that directs you to other topics. For Business ethics, the "see also" card suggests that you look into Businesspeople, Business, Professional ethics, Social ethics, and Industry—social aspects.

Once you finish with the card catalog, move on to the periodical section. Search through periodical indexes, using the same topic headings you used for the card catalog search.

Example 8.3 shows the style used for bibliography cards in magazine or periodical news articles.

A magazine or periodical card contains a subject indicator, the

EXAMPLE

8.2

174.4   Business Ethics
H517

Private Keepers of the Public Interest

Paul T. Heyne

N.Y. McGraw-Hill, 1968

EXAMPLE

8.3

Ethics in Industry

R. C. Wilson
"Industrial Integrity—America's Future"
December 11, 1979
Vital Speeches 46: 284–7, F 15 '80

author's name and the title of the article, and the facts of publication. In Example 8.3, *Vital Speeches* is the name of the publication, 46 is the volume number, 284–7 is the page numbers on which the article appears, and F 15 '80 means February 15, 1980.

A news article card contains a subject indicator, the facts of publication, and the headline of the news article. In Example 8.4, (Mon) means Monday, Ja 3 means January 3, IV means section IV of the paper, and 4:5 is the pages on which the article appears.

EXAMPLE

8.4

N.Y. Times   Ethics—Accounting

"American Institute of CPA's propose guidelines
and govern independent auditors . . ."

(Mon) Ja 3, IV, 4:5

For some papers it is necessary to use reference sources such as encyclopedias, dictionaries, or bibliographies. These books can also help you find sources of information. If the subject calls for it, head for the reference room.

The best sources of information in the library are the librarians. Feel free to ask questions and ask for help. After all, it's their job.

For all your sources, however, make sure that they are fairly recent, say no more than twenty-five years old, and that they are well-documented. Books that are authoritative on a subject are well-indexed; the written material is well-footnoted and contains an extensive bibliography of its own sources.

To get started in the right direction on finding sources, ask the instructor or a librarian which author is the most well known in the topic area of your paper. Having some source material with the author's name and using the bibliography to find more sources usually gets bibliography building for a paper off to a good start.

As you might be able to see, putting the subject on bibliography cards is a beginning for thinking about the form or outline the paper will take. Headings suggest subtopics. Seeing topics and reflecting on subtopics helps suggest further sources to explore.

A Practice Exercise in Bibliography

Now it's your turn. Suppose you were to write a paper on "Water Pollution"

(or select a topic of your choice) _____. Go to the card catalog and select several sources under the main heading. Prepare a bibliography for at least three sources.

Now list the other possible topics under which you would find information: _____

_____

_____

Prepare bibliography cards from the possibilities listed under headings other than the main one.

What references does the "see also" card suggest you turn to?

_____   _____

_____

    Now head for the periodical room and locate at least three sources in journals or popular magazines and make bibliography cards for them.

Subject:

Author:

Title:

Facts of Publ:

Step 3: Making Notes from Reading Materials

Once you've gathered all the bibliographic references, it's time to sift through the sources to locate and make notes for the body of your paper.

For note-taking, use larger cards, either 4 by 6 or 5 by 8. Remember, each note should be made on a separate note card. If you take twelve notes from one source, use twelve cards.

Just as you read a text and take notes after reading, do the same when you take notes from sources for a term paper. It is necessary to get an overview of the source before you decide what notes to take. Since the books are all library-owned and you can't mark them up for notes, slip one of your note cards into the book at a spot from which you may want to copy a reference. After reading the section, chapter, or article, you can make a better decision.

In taking notes from library sources, you want to be both accurate and honest. Accuracy is important, because once the note is taken and the book put back on the shelf, you don't want (or have the time) to return to it again. Honesty is important because you are using material written by another person. You are responsible for proper documentation, giving the author credit for the ideas you use in your paper. Not giving credit to a source or idea that is not your own is called plagiarism. Instructors are fairly familiar with most sources in their areas of expertise. If they see an undocumented idea that they know belongs to someone else, it is liable to result in a lowered or unacceptable grade for your paper. In addition, you cannot ignore or omit information which might be contrary to your thesis. The reader expects to see both sides of an issue or question.

What does a note card look like? A note card contains the author's name or other identifying tag in the upper left-hand corner. You can also use the name of the book or article to identify the source.

In the right-hand corner, use a tag identifying the topic or the subject of the note. The body of the card contains the note itself—a quote, a paraphrase or summary, an outline, a combination of any of the above, or a personal observation. For a quote or paraphrase, be sure to include a location for the source—the page on which it can be found in the book or article. A rough layout of a note card is shown in Example 8.5

What kind of notes should you take? This will depend on the paper, but you should get the right kind of material and a good variety of it.

EXAMPLE

8.5

Author	Subject of Note
Body of Note	
	Page number

Nonevaluative studies require facts and information regarding the treatment of the subject by others, but evaluative studies require both facts and opinions. If research data are included, you must learn to note the methods, procedures, and conclusions. In any case, notes fall into several major categories.

QUOTATIONS
Quotes from an authoritative source are necessary to give a paper credence. Use a quote when you want to be very accurate about your information or when the author has said what you want to say in a much better way than you could. Since the author is an expert in the field, his or her precise language will help give your paper validity.

A quotation note card (see Example 8.6) contains an identifying tag for both the author and subject, the direct quote, and the page number on which it was found.

EXAMPLE

8.6

D. Steinhoff	Opinion on <u>Depreciation Methods</u>

"The best authorities in the field will usually admit that depreciation methods are only intelligent guesses at best."

page 274

PARAPHRASES OR SUMMARIES
Paraphrases summarize or abstract ideas from a source. After reading a page or chapter, put the author's ideas which you want to use into your own words. Since you are taking someone else's ideas, it is necessary to acknowledge that fact. If you don't, it is plagiarism. A paraphrase note card contains an identifying tag for both the author and subject of the material, the paraphrase or summary of the ideas, and the page number on which it was found (see Example 8.7).

EXAMPLE

8.7

D. Steinhoff   Depreciation Methods

"Although there are a variety of depreciation
methods that can be used, no one method is
best because at best they are all no more
than good guesses."

Page 274

OUTLINES

Some material you read would be considered common knowledge—
interesting but not original material that you may want to note for
background knowledge.

An outline note card contains an identifying tag for both the author
and subject of the material and the outline necessary for your paper (see
Example 8.8).

EXAMPLE

8.8

Steinhoff   Depreciation Methods

4 major methods of figuring depreciation:

    1. straight-line method
    2. use or production method
    3. declining-balance method
    4. sum of the years digits methods

PERSONAL OBSERVATIONS

Sometimes when you are reading, ideas pop into your head. They may refer to how you are going to present or deal with material, or they may be original thoughts about the content. In any case, they should be noted right away. It is a great help in the actual writing of a paper to have these personal notes. They can very well provide a direction or even the thesis for the entire paper.

A personal observation card contains an identifying tag referring to the author from whom the observation stems, a subject tag, and your personal observation (see Example 8.9).

EXAMPLE

8.9

Steinhoff	Depreciation Methods

If so many methods of depreciation can be used and no one is superior to another, isn't it possible that businesses either use the wrong one for their needs, or there could possibly be a lot of cheating going on?

COMBINATIONS

Occasionally, you will want to combine two or more of these kinds of note cards. For example, you may cite a quotation followed by a paraphrase of the rest of the material, or you may cite a quotation followed by a personal observation.

A combination note card contains an identifying tag for the author and subject of the material, your idea about the material, and the page number of the source if it is appropriate (see Example 8.10).

A PRACTICE EXERCISE IN MAKING NOTE CARDS

Using this book, one of your other textbooks, or a library book, make a sample note card for each of the categories cited above.

EXAMPLE

8.10

Steinhoff   Valuing Stock

There are several considerations in selecting a valuing method—
these are "expediency, tax considerations, operation results,
and the outlook for the future."

                                                   Page 266

Idea for Paper
Take these considerations and apply them to the 5 methods for
valuing inventories in a particular case study.

Quotation

Paraphrase

Outline

Personal Observation

Combination

Step 4: Giving Direction to the Paper: The Outline

To outline the paper, you will need all your note cards, some blank lined paper, and a pen or pencil.

The purpose of an outline is to produce an orderly, logical sequence of ideas from your research for the benefit of the reader.

The process of outlining is really a continuous one, beginning with the collection of bibliography and extending into the collection and labeling of notes from library sources. Throughout these two steps, you will be able to see the major and minor ideas of the subject emerging and developing.

Begin the outline by sorting through your note cards and putting all the cards with similar topic tags together. The cards should suggest the

EXAMPLE

8.11

Older Adults—31 to 60
    First school experiences
    Putting down roots (families, mortgage, etc.)
Awareness of Sexuality
Aged—60+
    Puberty
Growth Stages
    Personal relationships (marriage breakdown)
Limit Testing
    Retirement
    Further physical and/or mental decline
Young Adults—13 to 30
    Marriage?
Raising a Family
    Parenting—guiding next generation
    Sexual inadequacy
    Parenting one's parents
    Economic pressures
Family and Sibling Relationships
    Peer pressures
    Physical decline
    Choosing a career
    Adolescence
    Dealing with death—own
Childhood—0 to 13 years
Settling in a Career or Change It
    Identity
Learning to Be Intimate
    Loss of spouse
Myth of Sexual and Intellectual Debility
Sense of Immediacy
    Live in the here and now

major divisions of your paper. The process of sorting through your cards to locate topics will probably be repeated about four to five times, since it is fairly typical for the average ten-page college research paper to contain about four to five major ideas.

Labels from a set of note cards for a paper on "Challenging Tasks in the Stages of Human Development might look like the list in Example 8.11.

When they are organized, they should fall into four major groups:

Childhood—0 to 13 years

Young Adults—13 to 30

Older Adults—31 to 60

The Aged—60+

Each group would have its own set of tags drawn from the labels on your note cards, as shown in Example 8.12.

EXAMPLE

8.12

Childhood—0 to 13 years	Young Adults—13 to 30
Growth Stages	Adolescence
Family and Sibling Relationships	Identity
First School Experiences	Peer Pressures
Limit Testing	Learning to be Intimate
Puberty	Choosing a Career
Awareness of Sexuality	Marriage
	Raising a Family

Older Adults—31 to 60	The Aged—60+
Parenting—Guiding Next Generation	Retirement
Putting Down Roots (family, mortgage, etc.)	Further Physical and Mental Decline
Settling in a Career or Changing it	Dealing with Death—Own Loss of Spouse
Personal Relationships (marriage breakdown)	Myth of Sexual and Intellectual Debility
Economic Pressures	Sense of Immediacy—Living in the Here and Now
Sexual Inadequacy	
Physical Decline	
Parenting One's Parents	

Once you have the major topics selected and organized into the sequence in which you will present them, you can write a purpose statement for the paper.

Each of the five main topics should be used as a major part of the outline, and the note cards containing the information in each area should be arranged in order of presentation as supporting material. Unless you have to turn in an outline of the paper before writing it, a formal outline is not necessary. Your purpose is to give direction to the paper by setting up the order in which you want to use and present the material you so carefully collected. The reader needs order to fully comprehend the written word. If you write in an orderly fashion, the reader will perceive your paper in an orderly fashion. The outline is the means to that end.

Step 5: Writing the First Draft

For many students, writing anything, especially a formal research paper, is a fearful prospect. Blank paper strikes terror into the stoutest heart. Writing does not have to start at the beginning and proceed through to the final sentence. Even professional writers write what feels comfortable first and then proceed to the more difficult sections. Since your paper already has been broken down into small parts in the outline, begin by writing small sections at a time around the elements of the outline. When one section is complete, go on to another. Many writers save the thesis or opening paragraph till last; they feel that they have a better handle on the most important statement after they have dealt with and written about all the topics and information they have collected.

A rough draft is no time to worry about grammar, spelling, or sequence of ideas. It's a time to get words on paper as quickly as possible.

In the next phase of the process, you can worry about the refinements. If you handwrite the paper, use large sheets of lined paper and write on every second or third line. This generous use of space will give you room to make corrections, additions, or deletions easily and efficiently, without a lot of recopying. Pen is recommended over pencil since it makes the paper easier to reread during the editing process.

Some people can type and think or create at the same time. If you are one of those, rough-type the paper on large unlined sheets, typing on every third line to allow space for editing later.

As you write each section, be aware of the way in which you want to present the material. There are several basic methods of organization; the material itself should dictate the structure of presentation.

For example, in presenting historical or biographical data, you want to use a time order pattern, beginning with the earliest facts and working up to the present.

In presenting a description of a process (whether a scientific one such as photosynthesis or a democratic one such as electing a president) or the technical workings of machinery, use a step-by-step pattern, starting with the first step and proceeding through to the last one.

In presenting material related to a large geographical area, use an area-by-area pattern. For example, in discussing agricultural techniques used by farmers in the United States, you may want to present the data on a region-by-region basis: first the northeast, then the southeast, then the midwest, and so on.

Ideas can be presented in a general way and then followed by examples, or you can begin with examples and build to the major parts, drawing from all the supporting data.

For example, you may begin a psychology paper by stating that "Neurotics exhibit a wide range of behavior" and then go on to give examples of the behavior that support your thesis. On the other hand, you may cite the examples and end up by stating the generalization that "Neurotics exhibit a wide range of behavior."

Some data lend themselves to comparison of similarities, such as the preparation techniques of speeches and term papers. Or you can contrast differences, such as between studying a foreign language and almost any other college course.

As you write, you will want to footnote the quoted and paraphrased sources. Use bibliography cards to construct the references and note cards for page locations.

It is not necessary to be exact in numbering the footnotes at this time. That comes later in the editing process, when you assign each footnote a number in the proper sequential order. For the proper form to use for constructing both footnotes and bibliography, it is recommended that you purchase a guide to paper-writing and keep it on your personal library shelf. The college library, as well as the school's learning resource center, always has such reference works. Most of the reference books contain examples of the various forms of footnotes taken from a variety of sources (books, periodicals, etc.) and the placement of footnotes in a paper, as well as the arrangement, form, and content of a bibliography.

It is also suggested that you keep a grammar book on hand that demonstrates a variety of sentence patterns and explanations of a variety of common errors in usage, as well as a dictionary and thesaurus to help with accuracy and variety in selecting words for the paper.

Once you finish the rough draft, you will probably want to read it over to make sure it follows your outline and includes all the major parts with the appropriate support in details.

Now it's time to rest for a while. Put the paper away for two or three days. When you go back to edit it, you will have a sense of perspective and detachment.

Step 6: Editing the Paper

Editing a paper means going over it with a fine-tooth comb to check on its content, style, and format.

Since you put the paper away for several days, you now can read it as if it were new and unfamiliar, almost as if it were written by someone else.

Reading the paper out loud, or reading it into a tape recorder and listening to it as you edit, frequently points up errors in logic or grammar that might be missed when you read silently.

Begin the first reading with the purpose of checking on content and organization. Once again, make sure you have covered all the points in the outline. Make sure each point is clearly made and well-supported or documented. If you presented quoted evidence, see whether the quote is appropriate to the point being made. A research paper is not a sequence of quotes connected by a few sentences; it contains ideas gathered from your reading, supported by appropriate material from respected sources.

Look at the introduction and conclusion. Does the former state the thesis of your paper clearly and correctly? Does the latter summarize your thoughts and research evidence?

Next, reread the paper for style. Examine each paragraph. Locate the topic sentence and the supporting details. For beginning writers, it is easiest to begin a paragraph with a topic sentence and follow it with details. Rewrite any sentences that need to be corrected to add coherence to the paragraph and the paper. The space left between sentences makes this process easy.

Also make sure the paragraphs follow in logical order. Feel free to reorder the paragraphs if it would make more sense to have a later paragraph precede an earlier one.

It is suggested that you cut apart the paragraphs you want to rearrange from the rest of the paper and then staple or glue them to blank sheets of paper. This makes for much less confusion while you are typing and prevents the possibility of making a costly typing error that might throw off the whole scheme of the paper.

As you read the paragraphs, sentences, and words, check for repetition of ideas and vocabulary.

Finally, reread the paper and put the footnotes and bibliography in final form, assigning numbers to the footnotes and alphabetizing the bibliography cards.

Step 7: Typing the Paper

Typing is an essential element in the preparation of a term paper. If you do not know how to type, you will have to prepare the paper several days ahead of schedule and give it to a typist. It's a good idea to locate one well ahead of time and contract for the service in advance since the typist is likely to be another student who also has school and other work obligations to consider. If you use a professional, your paper will have to be scheduled along with those of other customers. If you wait till the last minute, your paper may be turned in late. In some instances, the grade drops one letter (say from B to C) as a penalty for lateness. It's always a good idea to check this with the instructor beforehand. If you are a slow or inaccurate typist, give yourself several days to accomplish the task.

Once the paper is typed, proofread it carefully. Typing mistakes are just that—mistakes. You will be held accountable for all spelling errors.

Make sure you have included all the bibliography and footnotes and have not omitted any sentences, or even paragraphs, from the original version.

Some recommendations for typing are:

- Leave a 1-inch margin all around the paper, both left and right sides, top and bottom.

- Double-space the body of the paper.

- If a footnote is on the same page as the quotation, make a light pencil mark on the bottom of the page so that you will know when to stop typing the text and start typing the footnote. Many instructors allow you to type footnotes at the end of the paper. This is easier, especially for an inexperienced typist. Ask which form is most acceptable before proceeding.

- Use arabic numerals to number the pages.

- Type a title page with the title at the top and your name, the title of the course, and the due date of the paper at the bottom.

It's a fine feeling to complete a paper and know it's done several days before the deadline. Congratulations!

A FEW WORDS ABOUT GRAMMAR, STYLE, AND VOCABULARY

This section contains a list of suggestions regarding grammar, vocabulary, and style to consider when writing and proofreading a paper.

If you have never had a formal writing course, or if it's been a long time since you had one, it is strongly recommended that you take one. College-educated or not, every person has an obligation to know how to both read *and write* the English language.

There are several very common errors in grammar which you should be aware of in proofreading and editing a draft.

- Pronoun references must be clear enough so that the reader knows to whom or to what each refers.

- There must be proper agreement between subject and predicate.

- Sentences should be constructed in a parallel manner.

- The use of tense and person must be consistent.

If you are not sure of punctuation, for example, the many uses of the comma, consult a grammar handbook.

Sentences should be varied. To learn how to write simple, compound, complex, and parallel sentences, consult a grammar book. The most common error students make in sentence construction is using too many words. Any time you feel a sentence is too long, count the words and rewrite it. Use simple, active, direct sentences to avoid wordiness. For example, compare "It was voted that there" with "We voted," or "It is necessary to extinguish all incandescent illumination following the onset of nightfall" with "Turn the lights out after dark."

In vocabulary as well as sentence construction, you have to be concise and direct. Unnecessary or ambiguous words add to a paper's vagueness. Use specific nouns. For example, call an animal a Persian rather than a cat. If you use an abstract concept such as democracy, make sure you define it or provide examples so that the reader knows exactly what you mean. The language of a research paper is formal; therefore, clichés and catchwords should be avoided. No matter what your choice of words, make sure they are spelled correctly.

THEMES

Most students have had the experience of writing a theme before they take a college English class. As far back as the second grade, themes on "My Summer Vacation" or "My Pet" are common writing assignments. In college, theme-writing is an integral part of the basic freshman writing course. Usually through a combination of instruction and modeling by reading written examples, the techniques and types of themes are presented to the student. The purpose of the assignments is to have the student reproduce the model as closely as possible. Being educated implies being literate. Being literate implies the ability to express oneself accurately in the appropriate mode in the English language in order to be understood by the reader.

Most students do not enjoy basic college writing courses. Frequently, the ability to express themselves via the written word is at less than a college level. It seems to raise a lot of anger and resentment in students when they have to perform a task at which they feel less than proficient. Sometimes they blame their previous educational experience; their lack of knowledge of grammar, spelling, or punctuation; or themselves. Whatever the case, the ability to express oneself in writing is a mark of an educated person. Although you may not like it, it is necessary to learn how to do it. If you are angry because your previous writing experiences were poor ones, or if you ignored the instruction when it was given to you, freshman English is a time to reverse that attitude.

Regardless of whether your future circumstances will include heavy use of writing skills, being able to express yourself in written form is important. Most employers report back to colleges that the one skill they wish prospective employees had more of was the ability to use written communication. This statement is as applicable to those being employed at the managerial as it is to those at secretarial and clerical levels. Students in technical areas, such as math, engineering, or science have an even greater on-the-job need for writing skills than those in more traditionally liberal arts-oriented areas. Even if your future writing goes only as far as expressing your dissatisfaction as a consumer or communicating with distant friends or relatives, it must be done coherently.

What are your feelings about your writing experiences and skills?

My previous writing experiences have been _____

_____

_____

_____

My writing skills are _____

_____

_____

_____

In what future situations do you anticipate the need for clear, accurate

writing skills? _____

_____

_____

_____

The areas with which most students feel the greatest difficulty are selecting a subject and organizing a theme. Both of these will be discussed as part of the process of writing a theme.

THE TIME FACTOR IN WRITING A THEME

Themes usually are assigned three to five days before they are due. Frequently, these are weekly writing assignments. A final exam in a writing course will usually consist of constructing a theme during the exam time, anywhere from one to three hours. The time element is much more important for a theme than for a term paper. The necessity for breaking the task down stepwise and therefore timewise is obvious. If you have to write a theme every week, it can't be done at the expense of your other assignments or you will be playing catch up on homework all term long.

The next section will consist of the steps in writing a theme. First, let's fit those steps into a time frame, assuming a five-day time limit. As in the case of a term paper, an earlier mental deadline, say four days, will allow for the contingencies of life (see Example 8.13). Then let's take those same steps and assume a two-hour time limit for writing a "final" theme (see Example 8.14).

Most English courses focus on a few basic types of writing, which will be explained here. However, since this section is not a complete manual for writing, you will need to consult a writer's handbook or take a basic English course to really get into it.

Argumentative themes are just that—written statements arguing for or against an issue. It is necessary to convince or "tell" your point of view to the reader.

As with all themes, it includes a beginning or opening expressing your point of view and a brief summary of the points you will present.

Each succeeding paragraph is an expansion of one of the points in

EXAMPLE

8.13
Time frame for writing a theme

Steps in Writing a Theme	Time Frame: 4 Days
1. Select a subject	Monday: 1/2 hour
2. Search for sources— the idea page	Monday: 1 hour
3. Giving direction to the theme—organizing your ideas	Tuesday: 1/2 hour
4. Writing the first draft	Tuesday and Wednesday: approximately 1 hour each day
5. Editing the theme	Thursday: 1 hour
6. Typing the theme	Thursday: depends on your speed and accuracy

EXAMPLE

8.14
Steps in Writing a Theme   Time Frame: 2 Hours

1. Select a subject	10 minutes: less if assigned— then use time on steps 2, 3, 4, or 5
2. Search for sources—the idea page	15 minutes
3. Giving direction to the theme— organizing your ideas	15 minutes
4. Writing the first draft	1 hour
5. Editing the theme	20 minutes
6. Typing the theme	No time needed for in-class assignment situation

your argument. The whole theme is wrapped up with a final paragraph that is a strong statement summarizing and reflecting your point of view.

Descriptive themes are written statements that allow for the most creativity on the part of the writer. A descriptive theme deals with people, including appearance or perhaps character. Or it may be a profile which incorporates appearance plus character traits, places, or things.

The beginning paragraph usually involves an overall description of the person, place, or thing to be expanded on in the body of the theme. The various succeeding paragraphs deal with the individual aspects summarized in the first paragraph. The final paragraph should leave an overall picture of the person, place, or thing described.

Explanation themes are step-by-step descriptions of a process or a description of how to perform or construct something. The most common form of explanatory writing would be a recipe for cooking or baking. Explanation themes usually begin with a summary of what is to follow. Each succeeding paragraph explains the steps progressively. The final paragraph is brief and represents a concluding thought about the whole process, perhaps indicating the benefits to the person now that the process is over. In many English classes, critiques, reviews, and even business communication forms are also taught.

STEPS IN WRITING A THEME

Step 1: Selecting a Subject
Just as is the case with a term paper, topic selection for a theme has to be specific, not general. Similarly, the topic has to be one which interests you. It is also necessary to select a topic with which you are familiar. It is

difficult to persuade the reader by describing an event or place or explaining a process with which you have only fleeting familiarity. Since a theme is usually written without research but is based instead on personal experiences, opinions, or events, the topic must be chosen on the basis of what you already know. You can't convince someone that winter sports are more exhilarating than summer sports if you've not had the experiences necessary to make the argument and the paper come alive with the descriptions, feelings, and imagery associated with the cold-weather activities. If you are writing from other people's descriptions, it won't be a convincing argument.

Step 2: Searching for Sources

You are your own resource for the data and information contained in a theme. Basically, it is a process of brainstorming ideas relevant to the topic. During the time allotted for this step, carry around a notebook or sheet of paper. Every time you get an idea on the topic, write it down. You can also designate a specific time period for brainstorming. In general, however, the knowledge that you have a theme to write keeps the topic uppermost in your mind. At the oddest moments you may get a grand idea. Jot it down on the idea page. Relevance or quality is not the most important aspect here. Quantity of thought is.

The more ideas you have, the easier the paper will be to write. Remember what was said about a blank page. Themes don't originate out of thin air; they need ideas for fuel and for organization and coherence. Strive for at least ten or fifteen ideas on the blank page before beginning to organize your efforts to write a theme.

If you are writing an argumentative theme, you may divide the paper into pro and con sections. If you are writing a descriptive theme, list all your impressions, regardless of their relevance. If you are comparing two places or people, decide on the aspect you are describing and fill out the idea page accordingly.

It is not necessary to write whole sentences; phrases or key words are enough to trigger your thoughts and imagination when it is time to write.

Suppose you are assigned to write a theme describing a place you've visited. You select Hong Kong because it impressed you deeply. It's impossible to describe the whole place, and so you decide to limit your picture to a sketch of the varied scenes of the island that come to your mind. You could have chosen to describe the types of people or the various foods you found there. An idea page for such a paper might look like the one shown in Example 8.15.

EXAMPLE

8.15

IDEA PAGE. THEME: HONG KONG—REGION OF VARIED PICTURES

Harbor: boats (warships, cargo boats, junks, sampans, yachts, ferries)
Harbor lights at night: boats are moving lights
Outdoor stall markets: beautiful vegetables, live animals
Beautiful high-rise apartments
Hillside: terraced farms (rice)
Animal-driven plows (water oxen buffaloes)
Well-dressed people
Varied ethnic groups
Babies being bathed on sidewalks
Cats eating rice
Department stores
Open-air food markets
Tenements
Long bamboo poles between windows—line for drying wash
Stores: guarded by Sikhs with guns
Villages: women and children only—men at sea
Food smells
Tourists
Fine restaurants
Languages: varied sounds
Coca-Cola signs on village huts

A PRACTICE EXERCISE FOR AN IDEA PAGE
Now you brainstorm ideas for an explanatory paper on a subject of your choice. Be sure that it is something with which you are fairly familiar. Jot down all the ideas that come to mind about the subject.

Idea Page: Topic   _____

Step 3: Giving Direction to the Theme: Organizing Your Ideas
Good themes, like good term papers, require outlines. The organization for your theme will come from the jottings or idea page that you will organize or arrange into some kind of order.

Start reading through the idea page and then locate and mark those ideas which belong or fit together. Cross out the ideas that do not belong. One suggestion is to take a large sheet of blank paper, divide it into several columns, and put the ideas that belong together in each column. You can also use index cards or separate sheets of paper. In any case, the similar ideas should suggest the major divisions of the paper.

Going back to the example of a descriptive theme on the varied pictures Hong Kong conjures up, an organization of the ideas would be categorized into three major groups: Harbor Region, Native Region, and New Territories Region (see Example 8.16).

EXAMPLE 8.16

Harbor Region	Native Region
Boats (warships, cargo boats, junks, sampans, yachts, ferries)	Varied ethnic groups
	Languages: varied sounds
Lights at night: boats are moving lights	Tenements
	Open-air food markets
High-rise apartments	Cats eating rice
Well-dressed people	Babies being bathed on sidewalk
Tourists	Long bamboo poles for drying wash
Department stores guarded by Sikhs with guns	Food smells
Fine restaurants	

New Territories Region

Villages: women and children only—men at sea

Terraced farms: rice

Water buffalo plows

Beautiful green color

Coca-Cola signs on village huts

Your theme would begin with an overall description of Hong Kong that summarizes the facts related to the contrasting aspects of its geographical features. Each succeeding paragraph would paint a word picture of one of the three areas. The final statement would be an overall, general impression statement engendered by the description.

Now organize the information from your idea page. The major divisions of your paper are:

_____

_____

_____

Your outline would look like this:

Step 4: Writing the First Draft

The aim of writing, either a theme or a term paper, is to be understood by the reader.

Much of what has been said about writing a term paper is also true of writing a theme. Begin with an outline and start to write where you feel comfortable. This might mean starting with the conclusion, the pro or con statements in an argumentative theme, or one of your points in a descriptive theme. Just jump in and write. Don't worry about the refinements of grammar, spelling, or punctuation. That comes later.

The beginning of a theme is probably the most difficult part to write. Most students get stuck on the opening paragraph. Indeed, most professional writers find it the hardest part of their work. It is suggested that you save it till last when you are writing at your leisure, when you have three to five days to complete a theme. However, when you are writing in class and have one or two class periods to complete a theme, the beginning may be the best place to start. The opening is the eye-catcher, in which you must grab the reader's attention by revealing what you are going to say in the body of the paper. If you can't get around to it during a class or final exam assignment, you will omit the most important part of your paper, and your grade may suffer drastically.

Once you've finished the rough draft of your theme, you will want to read it to be sure it follows the outline and the type of organizational pattern you have selected. Go back to the various kinds of themes described earlier in this chapter and review them.

Now it's time to rest for a while. Don't rest for as long as when you write a term paper, but put the work aside for a while in order to gain some perspective on it when you return to edit it.

Step 5: Editing the Paper

Follow the same basic steps in editing a theme as you did in editing a term paper. Read it out loud to check the content and organization of ideas. Next, reread it for paragraph style, which includes sentence sense, vocabulary, grammar, spelling, and punctuation.

Step 6: Typing the Paper

Typing will be possible only for themes you do outside of class. Reread the paper for errors after you type it.

When you write a theme in class, it will have to be handwritten, possibly on special theme paper. Check with your instructor and/or bookstore for any requirements.

The same caution made for writing essays applies to writing themes: Make sure your handwriting is neat and legible. The difference between a good and a not-so-good grade on a theme can be the reader's ability to get through the paper with ease rather than struggling to figure out what some poor specimen of handwriting is trying to communicate.

OTHER COLLEGE WRITING TASKS

While term papers and themes may constitute the bulk of college writing, there are other assignments that call for you to put pen to paper.

Autobiographies and Journals

Courses in communications, both personal and interpersonal; some psychology and sociology classes, such as courtship and marriage, history of the family, or human sexuality; and many personal development courses require that you write autobiographies and/or keep journals. In most instances, the instructors will supply a form or list of questions they want you to answer about your life. In the case of a journal, you may have to write entries on a daily or weekly basis. In some courses, the writing may be strictly a record of your impressions; in others, it may be a set of comments related to a topic, such as noting examples of good and poor assertiveness techniques used by yourself or observed in the behavior of others during the course of a week.

Book Reports

Any course that assigns outside reading may also require a book report. Usually it is a summary of your reading. You may also be asked to critique it—that is, evaluate it for its ideas—or compare or contrast it with information you are learning in the course or from another source.

In an English class, for example, you may be asked to demonstrate how a book exemplifies a specific writing style or period in literature. The purpose of the assignment is usually defined clearly by the instructor.

It is wise to get right on the assignment. Taking notes on the book while you are reading allows you to gather information and set up an outline, much as in term-paper writing. Since most students don't have time to read a book twice, especially an outside source, taking notes on 3 by 5 cards while you read helps you concentrate on the reading process and provides the material for the report. Assign a time frame to the book report, much as you would for a term paper.

Technical Writing

Science classes or technically oriented classes such as mechanical drawing or dietetics and foods courses usually require the writing up of experiments or the explanation of drawings that go with projects. Writing up a lab report for a science class will be discussed in Chapter 11.

Technical writing that accompanies projects usually involves explanatory writing, describing in detail the step-by-step process or reasoning involved behind the procedure or accompanying the drawings that you are presenting.

SUMMARY

Papers and themes are similar in that they both require:
  —Careful planning and sticking to a time schedule in order to complete the writing without interfering with other obligations
  —Careful choice of a subject
  —Careful selection of appropriate and relevant information, either from books or from your own thoughts
  —The making of an outline to organize your ideas
  —A rough draft
  —Careful editing
  —The presentation of a neat, logically organized, grammatically correct paper
  However, term papers and themes are different in that:
  —Term papers are usually written over a much longer time period than themes.
  —Term papers require library sources to support your ideas, while a theme's sources come from your own experiences, thoughts, attitudes, etc.

USING THE LIBRARY | 9

This chapter deals with the organization, services, and materials of a library. The organization and materials aspects are discussed further, with explanations of the three main sections of the library—the card catalog, the reference section, and the periodical section. Some representative materials contained in each are presented. The chapter ends with a hands-on library exercise meant to familiarize you with the layout and some of the basic materials in a library.

What kinds of experiences have you had in using a library?

_____

_____

_____

What are some of the questions you have on the use and functions of a

library? _____

_____

_____

_____

Therefore, based on your experiences in using libraries and questions regarding the functions of a library, the kinds of information you will want

to pay particular attention to while reading this chapter are _____

_____

_____

_____

Books have been with us a long time. Since people first began to write and record their histories on rock, clay, and wood, there has been a need to preserve and store the writing for the future. As long as there have been books, there have been libraries.

School libraries are places where learning materials in the form of books, periodicals, pamphlets, audiovisual aids, etc., are kept. Using the library is a way of making the materials necessary for learning easily accessible.

Many students have not had extensive experience using a library, having gone through high school, and perhaps most of their adult life, without stepping inside one.

Just to dispel any rumors, libraries are neither scary nor difficult places in which to find learning materials or research a term paper. They are arranged logically for ease of locating books and periodicals, and they contain some of the most helpful people on campus—librarians.

This chapter explains how libraries are organized and then goes on to explain how the books are organized within a library. Finally, it explains the function of, and describes particular materials in, both the reference and periodical sections.

Just reading the chapter without going to the library to investigate the material personally would be confusing and futile. Therefore, the final section is a hands-on library exercise which will allow you to come in contact with many of the materials described.

HOW LIBRARIES ARE ORGANIZED

Whether the library you use is large or small, it is basically organized with the same component parts. If your library is large, it may be housed in more than one building, being spread around the campus in small, highly specialized parts, such as an art or music or engineering library in the appropriate buildings. If your library is small, it is probably contained in a single unit, with all the parts and services in one central location.

The Parts of a Library

Almost every library has a main desk. In small libraries it serves many functions. You can use it to:

- Ask questions about the library
- Seek help in locating information
- Check out and return materials

In larger libraries, the main desk serves only as an information area.

There is usually another desk, called a circulation desk, that functions as the place where you go through the process of borrowing and returning books.

Every library has stacks or shelves in which the material or books are stored. In some libraries they are open areas. That means that you can browse through them at your leisure to locate books or with the help of a call number get the book you want by yourself.

In other libraries there are closed stacks. That means you can borrow a book only by presenting a call slip to a librarian or an assistant, who will get the book for you. Call slips contain the name and author of the book as well as the call number. Open shelves are always more useful than closed ones because they allow you to look through material and do a more careful job selecting books before you check them out. Frequently, other bookshelves near the subject area in which you are looking provide further sources of information not run across in the card catalog.

Most libraries also have reserve sections, areas in which you can find the collateral books and articles your instructors wish you to read. The material in these rooms changes from term to term, depending on the courses being taught that require extra or reserve reading. These are usually books or articles which your instructor feels will add to the information you are given in the texts and lectures. Reserve books do not circulate, and so you will have to read them in the library during a specific time period, usually two hours at a time. Frequently, reserve books are lent out overnight at the end of the day or for a weekend starting late on Friday night or Saturday afternoon. They have to be returned promptly the next morning or early Monday if they are lent out for the weekend. Since the library usually has only one copy of the material, promptness in returning it is important so that other students in the class can take their turn at the assignment.

Most libraries also have reading or study rooms that students can use to do library or other homework assignments. In some cases, there are quiet study areas where talking is not permitted and open areas where it is. The choice is yours.

Materials Found in Libraries

Most of the materials found in a library are housed in separate sections.

The card catalog is the major resource for locating books in a library. It is usually in a very accessible area, frequently near the main desk. Every book contained in the library is listed in the card catalog in three ways: by author, by title, and by subject matter. The call number on the card is an indicator of where the book is located.

Periodical rooms or sections contain current as well as back issues of material published on a regular basis, including newspapers, magazines, journals, and bulletins, which appear daily, weekly, monthly, or quarterly.

Reference rooms or sections contain highly specialized books of information. These include dictionaries, atlases, encyclopedias, gazetteers, bibliographies, and bibliographies of bibliographies.

None of the material in a reference room can be checked out. A reference librarian—someone familiar with locating information from reference sources—is the best person to ask for help when you need assistance with reference materials.

Material published by agencies of the United States government is found in special rooms or sections of large libraries, and in vertical file drawers in reference or periodical sections of smaller libraries. These are usually highly informative publications containing statistics, studies, or descriptions on a wide range of topics relevant to the agency which publishes them.

Many libraries also house audiovisual materials for some courses. This can include records and tapes of music or speech along with equipment for listening, maps, slides, filmstrips, and microfilms.

Many large schools also have rooms or sections which contain special collections of materials on a single subject area. For example, schools which specialize in medicine and train nurses, technicians, or even doctors may have special medical collections. Other examples would be special collections of Afro-American, Native American, or south or north Asian materials.

Services a Library Provides

Libraries provide a variety of services to assist their users in locating materials and researching papers. They also provide physical facilities to improve the efficiency of the student in using the library.

Most libraries contain duplicating facilities where you can copy materials from books and periodicals for use or inclusion in your papers. Some libraries have typing rooms with regular or coin-operated typewriters. Almost every library has study carrels, which are individual booths where a student can study. These are good aids to promoting concentration since they usually have front and side panels which make for privacy and few distractions, without leaving you feeling isolated. Some libraries have study carrels with doors for which a student can sign up over the course of a complete term. This can be helpful if you know that you will have consistent library work during a particular term or if you need a quiet place to study on a regular basis. Group study rooms are frequently available. These are small facilities containing a table, some chairs, and a chalk board which can be used by a group of students studying together. Many libraries, whether large or small, are tied in to other libraries by a computer system. If you are doing research for a term paper and come across a reference to a book you want to use that your library doesn't have, your library will search out a library that does have it and then borrow it for your use during a specified time period.

HOW THE LIBRARY IS ORGANIZED: THE CARD CATALOG

Once you know how your library is organized, finding materials won't be the hassle you may believe it to be.

All libraries are organized according to one of two plans, the Library of Congress system or the Dewey Decimal system. The purpose of the classification system is to provide a plan for organizing the material for fast and convenient use by the library user. It brings books on the same subject matter together for ease in storing on the shelves and for ease of retrieval.

Once you know which system your library uses, become familiar with the major categories of subject matter and the corresponding numbers or letters that make up the call numbers. This is especially true for your major area of study. Books on a particular subject are located in one section of the library. Knowing your area makes locating basic books easier. It is also good to know the other major areas in which you can locate information related to your field. For example, although the books you need for your major may be concerned with anthropology and are, therefore, in a particular section of the library, you also need to know in which sections books dealing with collaterally related material are found, such as psychology, religion, customs and folklore, agriculture, the arts, history, and geography.

A library that uses the Library of Congress system arranges its books by letters of the alphabet, with each letter representing one of the major divisions of the world of knowledge.

A	General works—Polygraphy	M	Music
B	Philosophy—Religion	N	Fine arts
C	History—Auxiliary sciences	P	Language and literature
D	History and topography (except America)	Q	Science
E–F	America	R	Medicine
G	Geography—anthropology	S	Agriculture—Plant and animal husbandry
H	Social sciences	T	Technology

J Political science

K Law

L Education

U Military science

V Naval science

Z Bibliography and library science

A library that uses the Dewey Decimal system arranges its books by numbers to represent each of the major divisions.

000–009	General works	Bibliographies, encyclopedias, etc.
100–199	Philosophy	
200–299	Religion	Bible, theology, etc.
300–399	Social sciences	Political science, economics, etc.
400–499	Language	Various languages, etc.
500–599	Pure science	Math, physics, chemistry, etc.
600–699	Applied science	Engineering, agriculture, etc.
700–799	Arts and recreation	Sculpture, painting, music, etc.
800–899	Literature	American, English, etc.
900–999	History	Geography, ancient and modern history, etc.

How Books Are Organized within the Card Catalog

Books are organized according to one of the systems described above, and both systems use a card catalog. The card catalog lists all books in the library alphabetically in three ways: by author, by subject, and by title.

Each card in the catalog, whether it is a title, author, or subject card, contains the following information:

1. The call number, made up of letters and numbers from one of the classification schemes. It describes the knowledge category that the book falls under and, therefore, indicates where the book is located on the shelf.

2. The author(s) or editor(s).

3. The title.

4. The publisher, place, and date of publication.

5. Cross-reference information which refers you to other subject headings in the card catalog to which you can refer for further information on the topic.

Examples 9.1, 9.2, and 9.3 represent the way the same book is catalogued according to the three types of library cards.

EXAMPLE

9.1

> En338.
>   F829
>
>
>   Fowler, John M.
>   Energy and the Environment—John M.
>   Fowler, N.Y.: McGraw-Hill, 1975.
>
>   XIV, 496p: 111, 24 cm
>
>   Bibliography, p. 485–488
>   Includes Index
>
>   1. Power sources   2. Pollution   I Title

AUTHOR CARD

EXAMPLE

9.2

>   Energy and the Environment
>
>   En338
>   F829   Fowler, John M.
>   Energy and the Environment: N.Y.,
>   McGraw-Hill, 1975.
>
>   XIV, 496 p: 111., 24 cm
>
>   Bibliography
>   Includes Index
>
>   1. Power Resources   2. Pollution   I Title

TITLE CARD

EXAMPLE

9.3

> Pollution
>
> En338
> F829
>
> Fowler, John M.
> Energy and the Environment—N.Y.:
> McGraw-Hill, 1975
>
> 496 p. 111: 24 cm
>
> Bibliography
> Includes Index
>
> 1. Power Resources   2. Pollution   I Title

SUBJECT CARD

The Reference Section

Reference books contain information. They are designed specifically for quick acquisition of specialized pieces of information. They are meant to be consulted, not read cover to cover.

Some reference books are general in nature and contain the information the researcher needs, such as dictionaries, encyclopedias, handbooks, and atlases. Some are more specific in nature and contain information that tells the researcher where to go to locate the specific information required, such as indexes, bibliographies, and directories. For example, to locate magazine or journal articles in the area of psychology, you would consult an index which contains lists of articles devoted to that subject.

Whether a reference book is general like a dictionary or specific like an index, it usually contains a guide to its information in the front. The guide tells you how the book is laid out (by topic, author, title, or all three) and what kind of symbols, abbreviations, or markings are used in listing each entry.

Some reference books are subject-specific; that is, they contain reference information only on a particular topic, such as business, art, psychology, or chemistry. Subject-specific reference books are the same as general field reference books, that is, dictionaries, indexes, bibliographies, encyclopedias, etc., as well as professional journals. For psychology, there is a dictionary of psychology, an encyclopedia of psychology, a bibliography of psychology, and an index and abstract of psychology as well as professional journals in psychology.

Some General Reference Books You Should Know

OXFORD ENGLISH DICTIONARY   There are many good dictionaries of the English language, but the *OED* is the grandparent of them all. It contains all the words currently used in the English language since the 1100s. Besides the usual dictionary entries, it also tells the derivation or history of each word.

ENCYCLOPEDIAS   *The Encyclopedia Americana* and the *Encyclopedia Britannica* are both written for the educated adult. Their articles are authoritative and complete. The *Americana* is especially good for science and technology articles. Since these articles are signed (the initials following the article belong to the writer), they are a good source of further bibliography. If you read a general encyclopedia article in selecting your subject, use the name of the author when you go to the card catalog to begin locating books for your paper. Each article is usually followed by a bibliography. Encyclopedias like *Colliers*, *World Book*, and *The Columbia Encyclopedia* are more general in nature and are written for the general public.

ATLASES   Atlases are books of maps. However, many contain a storehouse of other information.

   The National Geographic Atlas and *The Times Atlas of the World* are excellent sources for maps and geographical information.

   The National Atlas of the U.S.A. contains not only maps but charts, tables, and indexes of the physical features of this country as well as social, economic, historical, and political information.

HANDBOOKS, YEARBOOKS, AND ALMANACS   Handbooks, year-books, and almanacs give information in order to answer questions. You have to know whether your question involves an answer that needs statistics, summaries, historical or sociological information, etc., in order to select the proper reference work in this category.

   Many encyclopedias have yearbooks which list the events and developments of a specific year. For example, there is the *Americana Annual* and the *Britannica Book of the Year*.

   Both the *Information Please Almanac* and *The World Almanac and Book of Facts* contain world maps and factual information on a broad variety of subjects.

   Handbooks tend to deal with a specific subject, giving many small pieces of information on a variety of aspects of the topic. An example of a handbook would be Emily Post's *Etiquette*, which deals with the rules for social behavior. There are also handbooks in accounting, marketing, public relations, and secretarial science.

There are digests which condense a lot of information from a field, such as law, give summaries of plots of books, or digest large amounts of periodical information on a specific topic and present it in brief form.

BIBLIOGRAPHIES Bibliographies are books which contain lists of books. Some are general and have lists of books that are not limited to any one specific topic, author, or area of the world. Some are specific and contain works of a single type.

Bibliographical listings usually contain a general description of what is found in the book; in some cases the book is evaluated, providing a critical comment on its usefulness.

You are probably used to seeing bibliographies in your textbooks— the list of suggested readings at the end of a chapter or the end of the entire book is a bibliography. In addition to a book that has a bibliography for a specific content area, there are bibliographies of bibliographies, or books that list other books that list books. Got it? Some general bibliographies are:

A World Bibliography of Bibliographies

Booklist   A semimonthly list of recently published books

Books in Print   Published annually, it serves the same general function as *Booklist*.

Some Specific Reference Books You Should Know

Specific reference books fall in the same categories or general areas, such as dictionaries, encyclopedias, atlases, etc. The difference is that they pertain to specific subjects and are made to fit the needs of the subject matter. There are books of scientific tables, books of musical themes, and books of art reproductions.

Specific reference dictionaries, therefore, are concerned with giving definitions and sometimes chronological and biographical information on a specific subject. Some subject-specific dictionaries are:

The Dictionary of Psychology

The Dictionary of American Biography

The Dictionary of National Biography (Great Britain)

World Biography

Art Dictionary

Dictionary of World Literature

Specific encyclopedias give summaries of the various aspects of a subject and/or historical or chronological information on the subject. Some subject-specific encyclopedias are:

Encyclopedia of World Art

Encyclopedia of Jazz

The Encyclopedia of Chemistry

An Encyclopedia of Religion

Subject-specific handbooks and yearbooks perform the same function as general ones; they are sources of summaries, dates, quotes, plots, quotations, and statistics. Some subject-specific yearbooks and handbooks include:

The Secretary's Handbook

International Handbook of Universities

Handbook of Chemistry

The Statesman's Yearbook

The Yearbook of World Affairs

There are also subject-specific atlases such as the:

Atlas of American History

Advanced Atlas of Modern Geography

Specific bibliographies include:

Harvard List of Books in Psychology

Sources of Business Information

A Guide to the Literature of Chemistry

The Periodical Section
In addition to knowing how to locate information from the card catalog and reference sections of the library, you will have to be able to use the periodical section to find information in indexes to articles in periodicals, newspapers, and professional journals.

The periodical room has no catalog. It would be virtually impossible to catalog all the articles from the vast number of periodicals that are published. Therefore, to locate material in periodicals, you have to know and be able to use the various indexes.

Some indexes are general in that they list articles from nontechnical and nonprofessional publications, such as *Newsweek*, *Time*, etc. Others are subject-specific and list articles from professional and/or technical publications in specific subject areas, such as science, education, business, and law.

Indexes are usually arranged by subject, with the large topic listed first, followed by the various subdivisions of the topic. Take the topic "Drug Use and Abuse." In the *Readers' Guide*, the subject headings and subheadings appear in the following way:

Drug abuse
    See also
        Drugs and children
        Drugs and women
        Drugs and youth
        Tranquilizing drugs

Drug industry

Drug research

Drug traffic

Drugs
    See also
        Amphetamines
        Antibiotics
        Hypnotics
        Tranquilizing drugs

Drugs and children

Drugs and women

Drugs and youth

In the front of each periodical index is a list of the publications whose articles are listed in the index. Along with this is a detailed list of the abbreviations used in constructing the entries. Basically, each entry in an index includes the subject, the title of the article, the author, whether the article has a bibliography or is illustrated, the name of the magazine in which the article appears, the facts of publication (date of publication and volume number of the magazine), and the pages on which the article appears.

Example 9.4 shows a sample entry from a periodical index.

EXAMPLE

9.4

"Quick Fix for a Frustrating Problem" excerpt from *The Tranquilizing of America* R. Hughes and R. Browin. *Sci Dig* 87:43 March '80.

The entry gives the name of the article, the names of the authors, the publication in which it appears (*Science Digest*), the volume number of the magazine (87), the page on which the article appears (page 43), and the date the magazine was published (March 1980).

Note that the entry lets you know that this article is an excerpt from a book.

Some general periodical indexes are:

Readers' Guide To Periodical Literature, published twice a month, with material listed by author, subject, and sometimes title. About 100 general and nontechnical periodicals are represented, giving references to poems, plays, articles, and books.

New York Times Index, published twice a month, with material listed by subject only. Only articles, book reviews, and essays published in *The New York Times* are included. In order to find articles on similar subjects in local newspapers, one would go to the *Times* index, locate the topic and date on which an article appeared in the *Times*, and then go to the local paper for a comparable time period to find its article on the same subject. Some specific periodical indexes are:

Applied Science and Technology Index, published monthly and organized by subject heading. Some 200 pure and applied science periodicals are indexed.

International Index, published quarterly and organized by author and subject headings. About 170 journals containing social science and humanities articles are indexed.

Business Periodical Index, published monthly and organized by subject heading. An index to periodicals in the business and trade areas.

A LIBRARY SKILLS EXERCISE

The best way to get to know your library and its vast resources is to go there and put your hands on the books. The following exercise is designed to get you familiar with the library you use.

1. Where is your library located? _____

2. What days and hours is it open? _____

_____

3. What classification system does it use? _____

4. Are the bookshelves open _____ or closed _____ stacks?

5. Are the main information desk and circulation desk one and the same

_____ or different _____?

6. Does the library print a guide to its use? Yes _____ No _____

7. What special sections or collections does your library have in addition to the usual catalog, reference, and periodical areas?

_____

_____

8. What services does the library provide to students?

_____

_____

9. Begin at the card catalog. Select a book from an author card and supply the following information:

   Call number _____

   Title _____

   Author _____

   Place of publication _____

   Publisher _____

   Date of publication _____

   Subjects the book treats _____

   Any other information you think is important _____

   _____

10. Now select a general topic, preferably one from a course you are taking, such as chemistry, accounting, study skills, etc. By what

    name is the general subject listed in the card catalog? _____
    If it is subdivided into more specific areas, list them:

    _____

11. Name at least three books listed in this subject area that will give you

    background information for your course: _____

    _____

What items on each of the three cards you selected enable you to find additional information related to the topic?

_____

_____

12. Select a book title with which you are familiar and then look up the book by locating the title card in the catalog. Suggestions:
    Huckleberry Finn
    The Assertive Woman
    A Separate Peace

Reference Sources

13. Locate the _Oxford English Dictionary_ in the reference section of your library. Look up a word and trace its origin. Word: _____

    Origin: _____

    _____

14. Select a subject with which you are familiar and look it up in the _Encyclopedia Americana_ or the _Encyclopedia Britannica_.

    Subject _____

    Was the article signed? _____

    Who is the author? _____

    How many items were in the bibliography? _____

    How much knowledge of the subject does the article assume? ___

    _____

15. Select an encyclopedia that connects with a subject you are studying or would like to study. Browse through the encyclopedia at your leisure.

16. Find _The Dictionary of American Biography_, Vol. V. Look up the name

    Sarah Orne Jewett. What are her dates? _____

    Briefly trace her biography. _____

    _____

    _____

    _____

    What names does the bibliography suggest for further reference?

    _____

17. Locate the publication *Booklist*. Select a subject.

    _____

    How many books were published in that area during the period the

    bibliography covers? _____
18. Locate a handbook in an area you are studying or would like to study. Browse through it at your leisure.

Periodicals
19. Select a topic, or several topics, and locate an entry for the subject in each of the indexes cited in the organizational table.

	READERS' GUIDE TO PERIODICAL LITERATURE	EDUCATION INDEX	SOCIAL SCIENCE AND HUMANITIES INDEX	SPECIFIC SUBJECT INDEX OF YOUR CHOICE
Topic				
Author of article				
Title of article				
Periodical				
Volume				
Page(s)				
Date				
Other information				

SUMMARY

— Libraries are not complicated places if you know how they are organized, what services they provide, and the names and functions of some basic reference and periodical materials, as well as the card catalog.

THE
EFFICIENT LEARNER:
SPECIFIC CONTENT
STUDY SKILLS

III

STUDYING THE SOCIAL SCIENCES | 10

This chapter is concerned with studying social science course material. The social sciences include history, political science, economics, sociology, anthropology, and psychology. After a description of the content of the social sciences, the various study techniques are described, as well as the styles of writing employed by social science authors.

Mentally review your experiences with and knowledge of social science course content. If you have not had a social science course before, review your experiences with reading this type of material in newspapers and magazines. Then complete the following statement:

When I read or study social science type content, I ＿＿＿＿＿＿＿

＿＿＿＿＿＿＿＿＿＿＿＿＿＿＿＿＿＿＿＿＿＿＿＿＿＿＿＿＿

＿＿＿＿＿＿＿＿＿＿＿＿＿＿＿＿＿＿＿＿＿＿＿＿＿＿＿＿＿

＿＿＿＿＿＿＿＿＿＿＿＿＿＿＿＿＿＿＿＿＿＿＿＿＿＿＿＿＿

Therefore, based on my experiences, in order to get the most from this chapter, I will want to learn about and pay particular attention to

＿＿＿＿＿＿＿＿＿＿＿＿＿＿＿＿＿＿＿＿＿＿＿＿＿＿＿＿＿

＿＿＿＿＿＿＿＿＿＿＿＿＿＿＿＿＿＿＿＿＿＿＿＿＿＿＿＿＿

＿＿＿＿＿＿＿＿＿＿＿＿＿＿＿＿＿＿＿＿＿＿＿＿＿＿＿＿＿

The social sciences are concerned with the subject matter most dear to our hearts—ourselves. History is the story of the various peoples of the world—their struggles, triumphs, conquests, wars, rebellions, and ideas. Political science and economics deal with the political and economic institutions of people—their governments and laws, their use and misuse of economic human resources, and their political and economic struggles to gain freedom or peace or to repress or overcome others.

Reading social science content is like reading a newspaper. The events and people are not unlike today's events and people; only the dates are different. Through reading history, political science, or economics, we get an idea of how things came to be as they are today. By knowing the history of the Constitution, for example, we can gain a better understanding of the present-day problems we encounter when people challenge it or try to amend it.

Sociology, anthropology, and psychology are concerned with the social, cultural, and behavioral aspects of human beings. Sociology is concerned with the institutions by which society is organized. It tries to relate information on the various communities people form, such as families and social and business organizations; the behavior of people in groups; and the elements of social change. Anthropology deals with peoples other than ourselves; it examines the concepts, customs, rules, and mores that make up the thinking and social organization of different societies. Psychology is the study of people and their behavior in relation to the environment in which they live—how people learn, adapt, perceive, and solve problems. As you can see, the three are closely related.

Reading sociology, anthropology, or psychology helps us understand more about ourselves and others—how we function, and why we do (or do not do) the things we do. For example, it was mentioned earlier that one area of psychology is concerned with learning. Reading material on the psychology of learning gives people a good idea of what they are doing and why as well as what they should be doing to be more effective learners. Anthropology gives us ideas on why and how people of other cultures are like and unlike ourselves. As a result, we understand others so that when we meet them on campus or as businesspeople, teachers, or tourists, we can understand their speech and actions and can talk and act with intelligence, understanding, and compassion.

Social science courses form a large part of any academic curriculum, either as part of a general liberal arts program or as electives in professional programs. They are a vital part of human education.

SOCIAL SCIENCE STUDY TECHNIQUES

Social science courses are concerned with facts and ideas presented in the form of lectures, text reading, and other written sources the instructor feels will offer valuable material.

Lectures

As in any other subject, it is a good idea not to go to a lecture in the social sciences unprepared. That means having read the assignment or at least previewing it for the ideas it presents. It means reading the summary if there is one, looking at all the chapter headings and section subheadings, and perhaps skimming the more important paragraphs. Doing this will help you determine the purpose of the lecture, whether it is to explain or supplement the text material. In sociology and anthropology, it is common for the lecturer to use case studies and films to expand and exemplify the text concepts. In history, political science, and economics, it is more usual for the instructor to deal directly with the material in the book. In either case, if you don't know what's in the book, it's hard to tell what the lecturer is trying to accomplish and what you must get down in your notes.

Always edit social science lecture notes after each class, using your text as the first source for filling in missing or misunderstood material. In a history lecture, it is not uncommon for the instructor to jump around, covering many aspects of one historical period or event. Edit your notes to reflect the chronological sequence of events, or put all the facts about a person or idea together in the margin.

Courses in sociology, anthropology, and psychology include a lot of terms or concepts, and each one is usually illustrated by a case study or other example. Make sure that your editing reflects an understanding of the vocabulary of the course with appropriate examples.

Vocabulary

As was just stated above, knowing the vocabulary is a key to understanding a social science course and its content. Many of the words are familiar ones, but they are used to mean something specific and usually different from the meaning you are accustomed to. For example, you usually associate the word "drive" with a car or perhaps with ambition. In psychology, "drive" refers to the first stage of the motivational cycle, the stage at which an organism is impelled to action.

There are important root words in the social sciences which have a consistent meaning whenever we see them, whether they stand alone or as part of another word. In psychology, the words "cognition" and "cognitive" refer to the mental processes, such as thinking, remembering, planning, etc. Any time these words appear, either alone or in conjunction with other words, they refer to the same thing. Thus, you will find cognitive abilities, cognitive dissonance, cognitive learning, cognitive map, cognitive processes, cognitive psychology, cognitive slippage, cognitive stage, and cognitive theory.

In all the social sciences, there are roots or prefixes which are associated with particular subject areas. Certain prefixes provide a clue to everyday words and their meanings. If you know that re means "again," when you see the words return, remove, resist, replace, etc., the meaning is clear. Once you know that the stem *neuro* means "nerves" or "connected with the nervous system," anytime you see a word in a psychology text with that prefix, you will understand its meaning. For example, from the vocabulary of psychology, the root *neuro* is used in neurobiology, neuralgia, neuromuscular junction, neurons, neurosis, and neurotransmitter.

Learn social science vocabulary as you encounter it in your texts. Many texts have glossaries or dictionaries at the end of each chapter. Make a flash card for each new term, especially if it appears in the glossary. If there are a string of words associated with a prefix, you can put them all on one vocabulary card. Vocabulary learned promptly makes for easier reading and understanding of the course content. Making flash cards gives you practice in writing and defining the words; it's easy to carry the cards with you for quick, well-spaced study sessions.

Reading
Study techniques for reading social science materials are not unlike the techniques used for other subjects. The volume of reading, however, makes it especially necessary to space out your reading over time rather than cram it into a few study sessions. The denseness of the material—all the facts and the ideas which they support—is more easily dealt with if the task of reading an assignment is broken down into parts. A typical social science assignment can consist of several chapters, each anywhere from twenty-five to forty pages in length.

Let's say you have two chapters totaling eighty pages to read in one week. The most efficient way to handle it would be to read about ten to twelve pages a day each day for a week. This is especially important if you have another social science course at the same time or a math course which demands daily work. Saving the whole assignment for a single day can result in non-completion of the entire assignment, poor understanding, or the development of a distaste for the subject.

Use the technique discussed in Chapter 5 to preview the chapter. Read small sections of the material at a time and always question what you read and recite it in your own words before underlining, outlining, or making an organizational table or factual flash cards. Which retention methods you use will depend on the lecturer and the direction the course takes as well as the nature of the material. For example, vocabulary might best be put on flash cards, chronological and detailed material might best be outlined, arguments that present a pro and con view might best be underlined, and comparison and contrast might best be done in an organizational table.

If the lecturer follows the book or supplements it with stories or case studies, you may want to underline it or outline it and follow your notes during the lecture, putting in only the additional material discussed and highlighting the points the lecturer stresses. However, if the lecturer gives material not covered in the book, you will want to take good notes on the lecture and then integrate them with your notes from the text during the editing process. The bottom line on this whole discussion is that you need to use a variety of study techniques to suit the material you are reading as well as help stimulate and maintain your interest in the subject.

The facts and ideas you read in the social sciences are presented in a variety of ways. These ways were already alluded to in conjunction with the information on retention techniques. The following paragraphs explain each of the techniques social science writers use. When you ask yourself the question, How did the author say it? you can answer, "By defining, by giving details, by giving opposing facts or ideas, by showing a cause and effect relationship, or by giving an opinion."

Definitions

The vast number of new terms in the social sciences makes it necessary for the authors to frequently define the words they are using. This can be done in a variety of ways. Sometimes the author gives a direct definition of the word when it appears in the text for the first time. See Example 10.1.

In Example 10.1, the definitions sound as if they came from a

EXAMPLE

10.1

Retroactive inhibition is the opposite of proactive inhibition since in this case new learning and experience interferes with previous learning.

or

Social scientists from a variety of fields seem to agree that attitude could be seen as a predisposition to respond in a favorable or unfavorable way to objects, persons, concepts, or whatever.

(*Source:* M. Levin, *Psychology: A Biographical Approach*, McGraw-Hill, 1978, p. 268.)

dictionary. In Example 10.2, the experiment expands on the idea of modeling as a form of imitation. You are given not only a definition but an actual example of how it works.

EXAMPLE

10.2

Modeling is a form of imitation, and it is an important part of learning new behaviors. . . .

In one 1966 experiment designed to show vicarious learning, which is the experiencing of emotion through observation of others, Bandura had children watch a movie of an adult hitting and kicking a large rubber doll. Some children saw the adult punished for hitting the doll, others saw the adult rewarded, and a third group saw no consequences either way. After the viewing, the subjects were given the doll to play with, and they generally acted in accordance with their film's outcome. Those who had seen the adult rewarded were exceptionally harsh on the doll. . . .

(*Source:* M. Levin, *Psychology: A Biographical Approach*, McGraw-Hill, 1978, p. 450.)

Giving Details

In order to support or underline an idea, authors must present details—evidence that gives credence to their ideas. The evidence may be in the form of a list of facts, points, ideas, or implications. In Example 10.3, the author states that a variety of methods are used to gather data for job analysis. The obvious next step is for the writer to list those techniques.

In Example 10.4, the author includes a list to support the concept that individual differences are important in the job-selection process. However, instead of facts, a list of implications is presented, supplying logical connections between the concept of individual differences and their meaning for managers in the hiring or selection process. (Note how the word "implication" is defined within the context of the sentence.)

EXAMPLE

10.3

Sources and methods. The process of job analysis demands that we gather data about particular jobs and the kinds of things that people do to be successful in those jobs. The methods used to gather such data include a variety of techniques. We can observe individuals while they are actually performing their jobs. From these observations we could generate a description of the types of tasks performed by people in these positions. A film could provide us with similar information. Another frequently used source of data is the interview. One or more job incumbents can be asked to describe what they do on the job. A questionnaire is a somewhat more impersonal way to collect similar information. Finally, training manuals, reports, records, and other sources of available information may be appropriate.

(*Source:* T. R. Mitchell, *People in Organizations: Understanding Their Behavior*, McGraw-Hill, 1978, p. 333.)

EXAMPLE

10.4

The implications of this principle of individual variation are important for managers and the company as a whole. First, supervisors and subordinates must realize that there will always be some people who perform better than others. Not everyone can perform at the level of the best employee. By firing the worst performer you simply make another individual the worst performer in the group.

Similarly, if everyone is producing exactly the same amount, a supervisor should check for informal norms. The lack of variability is probably due to enforced norms concerning how much work should be done. Left to their own initiative or motivation, the individuals in the group would show some variability.

Individual differences are an important element for planning at the company-wide level as well. Different productivity rates result in different labor costs per unit and different overhead costs per unit. Also, the costs for selecting and training people for different jobs vary widely. It may be relatively easy and inexpensive to find and train a shipping-room packer, while an electronics engineer may cost 100 times as much to recruit and train.

Finally, from society's point of view, individual differences make up the human resources that keep the country going. People differ in their skills, potential, and actual performance. We have much talent and many different types of jobs, and the optimal match should be the mutual goal of both employees and management. People are happier and more productive when they are using their skills and talents.

(*Source:* T. R. Mitchell, *People in Organizations: Understanding Their Behavior*, McGraw-Hill, 1978, p. 333.)

Any time an author gives details or presents a list of ideas to support a statement, there are usually guideposts to look for. In Example 10.4, words such as "first," "similarly," "also," and "finally," give clues to the sequence of the material. Some other sequence or guide words in lists or arguments are "first," "second," "third," "in the first place," "then," "followed by," "next," "in conclusion," etc.

Opposing Facts or Ideas

Both facts and ideas are used in the social sciences to present opposing points of view when the author wishes to show the likeness or difference between two or more things, or to present two sides of an issue. In Example 10.5, the two houses of Congress and the membership, senators and House members, are being compared on several points: structure, power, knowledge, and work load.

In this passage, as each topic in the workings of Congress is discussed, the contrast between the senators and members of Congress is also made. The author, however, could have discussed all the topics

EXAMPLE

10.5

The Senate is the more prestigious of the two houses of Congress. It is also the more relaxed. Small enough to proceed without a great deal of formality. it can manage to have any or all its 100 members consulted on scheduling and procedural matters. The House of Representatives. on the other hand. is so large that it needs tightly structured procedures and a careful division of labor to get the work done. Its organization is more hierarchical. power is less evenly distributed. and it takes a member many years to rise toward the top. Power in the Senate is more evenly distributed. Democrats. for example. through a reform motivated by Lyndon Johnson as minority leader in 1953. are guaranteed a position on at least one major committee no matter how new and inexperienced they are. Pressure to conform is greater in the House than in the Senate. A senator has a national forum at his disposal from the moment he is sworn in. A member of the House finds it much more difficult to attain any kind of national visibility. He is therefore more dependent on his seniors.

House members. because there are more of them to share the work. are more likely to become subject-matter specialists than senators. A senator must divide his time among several committees and relies to a greater degree upon his staff for specialized knowledge.

(*Source:* D. J. Olson and P. Meyer, *Governing the United States: To Keep the Republic in its Third Century*, 2d ed., McGraw-Hill, 1978, p. 306.)

(structure, power, etc.) in relation to just one target—the senators, for example—and then gone on to discuss the same list of topics in relation to members of Congress. The end result would have been the same—a look at the workings of the Congress of the United States and how the two houses differ in regard to the same points.

In Example 10.6, the author is using ideas in a summary to point out the dichotomy or gap between what exists in fact and what the possibilities are, given the proper condition, namely, good use of resources and the development of satisfying organizations.

Notice that in this passage, as well as in the one about the Congress,

EXAMPLE

10.6

While the picture is not meant to be pessimistic. it is also not optimistic. Given more people who are better educated and want more meaningful jobs but are faced with diminishing resources. inflation, and high unemployment. the picture could hardly by glowing. On the other hand. if we intelligently use our resources and develop equitable and enriching organizational settings. progress can be made. The final chapter discusses some ways in which this process may come about.

(*Source:* T. R. Mitchell, *People in Organizations: Understanding Their Behavior*, McGraw-Hill, 1978, p. 415.)

the words "on the other hand" were used. That is an immediate clue to the presentation of opposing facts or ideas. Some other guide words to watch for in this type of writing would be:

While

Whereas

In comparison

Although

In contrast

Each of the words above indicates that it is only one part of a statement. Somewhere in the paragraph, chapter, or section, the other part of the story is presented. Further factual information, illustrations, or points of view are given.

Cause and Effect

Social science abounds with cause and effect writing. Authors are constantly trying to make the reader aware of the relationships between historical, cultural, social, or political events or concepts and people's or organizations' actions or reactions.

For example, in Example 10.7 from a political science text, the author is presenting the cause and effect relationship between a President and his or her image and what the effects of a lessened presidential image are on various peoples, the Congress, voters, and the economy.

It is not uncommon for history texts to deal heavily in cause and effect relationships. Every historical event was brought about by some precipitating cause, which in turn had an effect on the future. Similarly, both sociology and anthropology texts contain a lot of cause and effect writing.

EXAMPLE

10.7

Because presidential power is based largely on persuasion and expectations in the minds of others, much depends on the image the President presents to the outside world. The Nixon administration scandals, for example, quickly eroded the President's power base in all sorts of substantive areas which had no direct bearing on the scandals. Congress voted to curb his war-making powers because its members knew that a President with damaged personal prestige could not rally the voters to punish them at the polls. The economy, which is held together to a certain extent by faith, began to reflect investors' worries about uncertain leadership. This is an extreme example and one that cannot be. . . .

(*Source:* D. J. Olson and P. Meyer, *Governing the United States: To Keep the Republic in its Third Century*, 2d ed., McGraw-Hill, 1978, p. 348.)

Opinion

Both science and social science deal with facts. Scientific facts usually can be observed, measured, and quantified; in general, they are not disputed till they are disproved. The facts of social science, however, change with economic, social, and political conditions. This allows social scientists to interject interpretation, analysis, or opinion about what is occurring into their writings. These are statements which reflect the bias of the writer, and in most cases they will be clearly identified. For example, the writer in Example 10.8 clearly announces a bias in favor of a comparison between political and organizational institutions. The facts that describe political processes and those which describe organizational processes will be used to make the connections. In Example 10.9, the

EXAMPLE

10.8

A chapter on political processes is not included in most books on organizational behavior. For some reason the topic is usually avoided, probably because most people fail to see that organizations are political arenas just as governments are. Much of this chapter is designed to illustrate this similarity. We spend some time developing the idea that organizations are becoming increasingly concerned with the political support of their constituents. Systems of appeal are designed to combat managerial whim and capriciousness. Systems of participation tend to involve people in the legislative or decision-making processes of the organization. And finally. . . .

(*Source:* T. R. Mitchell, *People in Organizations: Understanding Their Behavior*, McGraw-Hill, 1978, p. 415.)

EXAMPLE

10.9

The fact remains that the science of human behavior is new. Relatively little is known about intrinsic freedom and dignity, or for that matter about how much controlling can really be done. Despite the criticism and praise lavished on B. F. Skinner, he is neither the ogre nor saint of his reputation. Rather, he is a man very much concerned with the present state of our civilization. He recognizes that neurotic behavior, alienation, crime, school dropout rates, unhappy family life, and the like are the result of defective social environments and he would like to do something about them. Although his theories may be oversimplified and his view narrow, underlying all his work is a question asked by philosophers and psychologists for centuries: Why be good, why tell the truth, what are the purposes of loyalty and honesty, why should anyone care whether or not the civilization or culture survives? Skinner's answer is that there is no real reason, but if your culture hasn't convinced you that there is, so much the worse for your culture.

(*Source:* M. Levin, *Psychology: A Biographical Approach*, McGraw-Hill, 1978, p. 268.)

writer has just completed a lengthy factual discussion of behaviorism, followed by a list of pros and cons about the study of human behavior from the Skinnerian point of view. The concluding paragraph is both a summation and a personal statement on the part of the author.

A FURTHER WORD ABOUT SOCIAL SCIENCE READING

In addition to your texts, many instructors in the social sciences like to supplement the information in a textbook with nontext reading. These are usually articles from newspapers or magazines, or sections, chapters, and even whole books written on one aspect of the course work. In anthropology, for example, it is common to be assigned articles and books that are complete descriptions of a particular culture. In history, there are often readings of documents or firsthand accounts of events peculiar to a particular historical occasion. Whatever the source, these writings usually contain the styles described above.

Frequently, these nontext readings are included in the book assigned as the course text. Often they are on reserve in the library. When they are on reserve, it will be necessary to:

- Plan time in your schedule to go to the library in order to do the reading well ahead of class time

- Plan to read and take notes on the material because you will be looking at it only once

What kind of notes you take on outside reading will depend on the reading itself and the purpose for the assignment. Usually, notes as detailed as you would take from your text are not necessary. Case studies and experiments for anthropology, sociology, or psychology require an outline of the problem, events, and results being presented. Readings on ideas, or commentaries for history or political science, require a summary type of note, with the general nature of the ideas or sequence of steps in a writer's thinking or argument being recorded.

The most important question, however, is how this outside reading contributes to the standard material being presented in the course. The answer should be a key determinant in your purpose for reading and the notes you take. Much of the content in social science is accompanied by maps or charts to illustrate or further explain the body of the text.

Maps are usually used in history to show the geographical area being discussed, perhaps to illustrate a country or countries' boundaries before and after a war or other historical event. Maps can also be useful in political science to illustrate political or demographic material discussed in the body of the text. The distribution of peoples or cultures can also be mapped in anthropology books.

Political science, sociology, and economics make heavy use of charts to illustrate or support the content with facts or studies. For example, in discussing taxation, an author may illustrate a point with a chart that shows the income of various levels of society, both before and after taxes, over a twenty-year period.

Whether your text has maps or charts or both, do not ignore them. Even if they only illustrate a point being made in the text, make sure you can state the purpose for the map or chart and recite what it says in your own words. Maps usually illustrate. Charts can illustrate, but they also compare or contrast. With a map you can say, "This map shows. . . ." With a chart you can also say, "This chart is comparing. . . ." Many of the newer social science books also contain cartoons or other illustrated materials taken from newspapers and magazines to further the author's point. Read them and make a connection between the illustration and the body of the text.

Exams

Social science instructors give both essay and multiple-choice exams. Regardless of the type of exam, they are concerned with the content of social science, that is, the facts, ideas, and vocabulary of the particular course. Studying, therefore, will involve learning chronological sequences of events; the reasons why (or why not) an event, a people, or an idea is the way it is or has evolved; comparing and contrasting events, people, or ideas; summarizing; and defining. The nature of the course, the type of exam, and the emphasis of the instructor will determine the what and how of your studying.

Regardless of the type of test, always try to attach the information you learn to an idea or concept. For example, just learning the amendments to the Constitution by rote will not be as useful as knowing the principles to which each is attached, and for what reason each amendment became part of the Constitution. In courses where maps or graphs form a large part of the explanation of the content, it is not unusual to find them on the test. You will either have to identify what is on the map or graph or, alternatively, provide the information by filling it in on a blank map or chart.

The principles of good exam preparation as outlined in pages 113 to 124 should be reviewed if necessary for application in social science courses.

Writing Papers

Social science courses frequently require you to write term papers. Instructors may or may not suggest the topic. What is always given, however, is ample time in which to complete the project and general instructions as to the nature of what is required, such as the use of primary sources or a bibliography and footnotes.

If you are not familiar with paper writing techniques, Chapter 8, pages 156 to 179, should serve as a guide to selecting a subject, finding information in the library, outlining, and writing the paper. As in writing any paper, the idea is to spread the work out over the time allotted, systematically chipping away at the various stages as you continue to go about performing everyday tasks at work, home, and school.

SUMMARY

— Social science courses are concerned with people—their history, culture, economics, politics, organizations, etc.
— Study techniques for the social sciences call for time-planning, adequate preparation for lectures, and a systematic approach to the text in order to handle the volume of reading which is characteristic of these courses.
— Learn the vocabulary connected with the social science course you are taking in order to understand both the lectures and the text.
— Social science writers use fairly consistent writing patterns to explain the content of their material. These include giving definitions, giving details, giving opposing facts or ideas to clarify a point, showing cause and effect relationships, and giving opinions.
— The principles of good exam preparation and the paper-writing techniques described earlier in this book apply to these two aspects of studying the social sciences.

STUDYING SCIENCE | 11

This chapter is concerned with techniques for studying science. After a brief description of the physical and life sciences, various strategies are discussed for studying the content as well as the styles of writing employed by authors of science textbooks to assist you in more efficient, effective reading of science material.

Mentally review your knowledge of and experiences with the content of science courses. If you have not had a science course, review your attitude toward the subject. Complete the following statements:

When I read or study science material, I _____

_____

_____

_____

My feelings toward the science courses I've had are _____

_____

_____

_____

Although I have never had a science course, I imagine _____

_____

_____

_____

Therefore, based on my experiences, in order to get the most from this chapter, I will want to learn about and pay particular attention to

_____

_____

_____

Science is divided into two categories: the life sciences, including biology, botany, physiology, and zoology; and the physical sciences, including chemistry, math, and physics. Some schools include physical geography in the latter group. The life sciences are concerned with living things—how they work, how they have evolved, and how they fit in with the environment around them. The physical sciences, on the other hand, are concerned with the properties, composition, structures, and functions of the energy, matter, and substances, both organic and inorganic, that make up the physical world in which we live.

Whether you take life science or physical science or both, it should be obvious from the nature of the material that science is concerned with questions. It is one area of the curriculum in which you can continuously use questioning techniques to understand the lectures, the texts, or the processes and results of lab experiments. Scientists constantly ask questions and find answers. Their writing is a record of the results. In order to understand the content of any science course, put yourself in the place of the scientist. As you listen, read, work problems, or do experiments in a lab, keep on questioning. Use all the levels of questioning discussed on pages 122 to 124—basic questions to recall facts, questions that will force you to recite material in more depth, and questions that will lead you to apply the facts in various situations.

For example, as a student in a dietetic tech program, you will have to take chemistry. The first question would be, How does this relate to me, and how will I be using it in my career? You have to know the basic facts of chemistry in relation to nutrients, for example. Basic factual questions deal with the properties, composition, functions, and structures of nutrients. In-depth questions focus on how the nutrients work in foods in relation to the human body, how much a person needs, and what occurs if a person has too much or too little of a particular nutrient, etc. Application questions are a technique that scientists use to formulate information; thus, it is the method you should use as a science student. It is a way to train your mind so that if you get stuck in learning or understanding, you can ask yourself what the appropriate question to ask in that situation would be. What did the scientist ask at this point in researching the subject that made an understanding of the process, structure, or events possible?

Beside fulfilling general educational requirements, science courses form a large part of the curriculum in many professional programs, such as nursing, dietetics, medical technology, and dental hygiene.

Like math courses, science courses are frequently seen as a major the successful completion of a program in higher education. manage to avoid taking science courses. Others take results that are less than satisfactory, and so they also have weak scientific backgrounds. Some students took science courses many years ago; although they did well, they realize that the content of and approach to science courses is quite different now from what it used to be. Regardless of the reason, a weak science background, like a weak math background, should be remedied.

If you have never had a science course, start simple. Many schools have multilevel science courses. For example, they may offer basic chemistry in several forms, with some sections meant for students who need to fulfill a requirement, and some meant for students in nursing or other medical programs in which the emphasis is different. A biology course to fulfill a requirement may be more concerned with how biology interfaces with the environment and society, whereas a biology course for nursing students may emphasize the physiological side of the subject.

Select your science course wisely. Find out what the instructor assumes you can do before entering the course. In basic chemistry and physics, it is usually assumed that you have had algebra and can work simple equations to solve the problems associated with the course content. If your math is weak or spotty, have a basic math book on hand that explains the general workings of equations. It is usually better to have completed algebra before attempting chemistry and physics.

In any case, seeking help will be up to you. Learning labs frequently employ tutors in basic science subjects or maintain lists of names of students willing to tutor others for a fee. If you had science courses a long time ago or did not do well in them, locate a good review book. Refresh your mind by looking through it before the course begins. Keep it on hand while you are taking the course to use as a back up when you need passages in the text explained in clearer, simpler language. As in any other subject, if you get stuck, ask an instructor, a lab assistant, or another student for help or clarification. Science courses are crowded with content, and it is important for you to understand the material as it is presented, since there is usually little time to return to material not thoroughly understood in the first place.

SCIENCE STUDY TECHNIQUES

Science courses are concerned with facts, theories, classifications, structures, properties, processes, and experiments presented in the form of lectures, text reading, and lab experiments.

Lectures

Science lectures are usually based on the material contained in the required text. Naturally, this implies preparation on your part before attending the lecture—previewing the chapter and acquainting yourself with the content of what will be discussed in the lecture. A good understanding of the text usually leads to a good understanding of the lecture. Once you have raised questions about the content in the text, listen actively in the lecture for your questions to be answered, or raise your hand to have the questions clarified. Some science students find that when the book and lecture are saying the same thing, they do better when they preview the book chapter, listen to the lecture, and then read the text chapter after the lecture. Obviously, this is an individual preference that works well in some cases but not so well in others. The choice is yours. The constant element in either case is the text preview in preparation for the lecture. If you read the text first and take good notes, your lecture notes will probably be brief and mainly on the points you missed or did not understand in the text. In the opposite situation, you will want to take notes from the lecture and then fill them in from the material in the book. In either case, notes for science courses are best taken on one side of the paper only, leaving the opposite page blank for editing, additions, diagrams, experimental evidence, and formulas that make notes complete and meaningful for study purposes.

Vocabulary

Science is loaded with vocabulary—specific terminology implying a precise meaning. Most science texts highlight new words by using italics or a larger or different color type. Frequently, the vocabulary is placed in a glossary either at the end of each chapter or the end of the book. If the vocabulary is at the end of the chapter, you should become familiar with the new words and their meanings before you read the chapter and definitely before you attend the lecture. If the vocabulary is highlighted in the chapter but not summarized at the end, go through the chapter and pick out the new words. In either case, vocabulary flash cards are probably the best way to learn science terminology. Flash cards made when you begin a new chapter ensure your awareness of the new terms.

Science vocabulary abounds in word roots—prefixes that are constant and provide meaning to the words in which they appear. For example, the prefix *ec* or *eco* literally means "house" or "environment in which something lives." A whole string of words beginning with *ec* or *eco* are related in meaning, e.g., ecology, ecological, ecosystem, etc. *Bio* means "life." When it precedes a word, it helps form the meaning of that word, e.g., biology (study of life), biocide (killing of living things), biofeedback, biodegradable, biogeographic, biome, biosphere, etc. Learn root words together.

ding is no more difficult than any other reading if you use
niques. The denseness of the material necessitates
ading, which implies proper scheduling of your time in

order to complete the assignments on time and in coordination with your other classes.

Science material cannot be read hastily. The intricate nature of the writing, including the many facts, descriptions, processes, and illustrations, requires a constant back and forth motion between the words and the illustrations. Without illustrations, science material would be meaningless. A discussion of the evolution of a particular process, the description of the structure of a plant cell, or the placement of the parts of a cell within an organism would be useless without drawings. Seeing the written material in pictures provides meaning to the words, which in turn enhances your understanding of the process or thing being described.

Visualization, then, is an important part of studying science texts. The book provides the words and pictures. Your job is to put them together, reading the words and seeing how the pictures illustrate them. The result should be understanding. When you are ready to learn or memorize the material again, combine the words and pictures. If, for example, you must learn the organs and their functions in the digestive system, draw the human figure, illustrate and label the parts of the digestive system, and talk to yourself all the time about the parts, their placement, and their purpose in the process. Your drawings do not have to be beautiful. They are a good functional learning tool, but one that works.

Science reading assignments vary in length, depending on the text and how fast the instructor goes in presenting the material. A schedule of daily reading is best. There is too much content in any one chapter to save it all for one sitting.

Notes from science texts will depend on the lectures and how they are integrated with the book. But there is no way you can read science without taking good notes.

The nature of science lends itself best to outlining, organizational tables, and factual note cards with pictures. The density of facts makes underlining in science texts difficult. It is not impossible, however. If you devise a successful system for underlining science texts, go right ahead and do it.

The nature of science dictates the patterns or ways in which authors of science texts present their materials. As in any other reading, when you recite the answer to the question, How did the author say it? you will want to be aware of the possible answers inherent in the nature of the writing. Scientists rely heavily on facts. They use facts to define terminology, explain processes, and show cause and effect relationships among scientific phenomena. The comparative nature of some aspects of science leads to the categorization of items, demonstrating how two or more groups or subgroups are similar or dissimilar. Science writers also describe experiments.

Definitions

Everything in science has a name. This accounts for the proliferation of terms. In Example 11.1, the author uses vocabulary to explain a process. In turn, the definitions of the terms come from the facts which describe their functions in the process.

Example 11.2 shows another way of using facts to explain a term.

EXAMPLE

11.1

In organisms with sexual reproduction, adult individuals produce sex cells. These sex cells are called gametes. Some organisms produce gametes that are all the same size; other organisms produce gametes of very different sizes. In these organisms, male gametes are called sperm and are small in comparison with the female gametes, which are called eggs or ova (singular, ovum). Sometimes, as in snails, one individual may produce both sperm and eggs: when this occurs in animals, these species are called hermaphroditic species. In higher plants (where male gametes are carried by pollen grains) individuals which bear both male and female flowers on the same individual plant are said to be monoecious. Plants which have flowers of different sexes on different plants are called dioecious. In the vertebrates, excluding the Agnatha and certain fishes, one individual can produce only one kind of gamete, either sperm or eggs, and is classified as male or female accordingly.

(*Source:* P. R. Ehrlich, R. W. Holm, and I. Brown, *Biology and Society*, McGraw-Hill, 1976, p. 209.)

EXAMPLE

11.2

Some insects and even some vertebrates can reproduce asexually. Aphid females may have daughters all summer long without mating and some species of lizards and fishes are all females. In such animals asexual reproduction involves development of eggs without true fertilization: This is called *parthenogenesis* or "virgin birth."

(*Source:* P. R. Ehrlich, R. W. Holm, and I. Brown, *Biology and Society*, McGraw-Hill, 1976, p. 209.)

Processes

Facts are also used to describe processes: how something in science
whether it is a description of the metamorphosis of a tadpole into a
ample 11.3, or the way in which magnets attract energy.
st read in a step-by-step frame of reference. The facts
r, with each fact being added on to the previous facts to
of how the event takes place. While you are reading the

paragraphs below, picture the process as a series of stages. Note that a picture accompanies the verbal description.

EXAMPLE

11.3

Distinct stages of development. Tadpoles are immature stages in the development of a frog or toad (see Fig. 6-26). The fertilized egg of a frog develops into an embryo, which gradually develops into a tadpole. Tadpoles have no legs, but they have well-developed tails with which they swim. Like fishes, they have gills for oxygen uptake. They eat algae and plant materials, living as tadpoles for a month to several years, depending upon the species.

Eventually a tadpole begins to change (see Fig. 6-26). Hind legs start to grow on each side of the body at the base of the tail. Front legs appear at the time the tail is gradually being absorbed and growing smaller and smaller. The tadpole then begins to breathe air as the gills stop functioning. It changes into an adult frog that spends part of its life on land and, as a carnivore, eats insects and other small animals. This remarkable change in structure, function, and way of life is called metamorphosis. It requires several weeks to several months in most frogs and is controlled by hormones from the thyroid gland.

(*Source:* P. R. Ehrlich, R. W. Holm, and I. Brown, *Biology and Society*, McGraw-Hill, 1976, p. 218.)

Cause and Effect

Sometimes facts are used to show the cause and effect relationship between scientific data and resulting events. Example 11.4 deals with how our weather is caused by the uneven heating of the earth by the sun and the effects it has on the hemispheres.

EXAMPLE

11.4

It is the angle at which the sun's rays hit different parts of the earth that primarily determines the differential heating. The closer to 90°, the more energy will be absorbed (Fig. 4-14) rather than reflected. Thus more energy is always absorbed near the equator than near the poles. And more energy is absorbed by the hemisphere tilted toward the sun than by the hemisphere pointed away from it. It is the different angles at which the sun's light hits the northern and southern hemispheres as the earth circles the sun that creates the seasons and makes them opposite in the two hemispheres. The importance of angle rather than distance from the sun is clear. The earth's path around the sun is not a circle, but an ellipse: winter in the northern hemisphere occurs when the earth is closer to the sun than it is in the northern summer!

(*Source:* P. R. Ehrlich, R. W. Holm, and I. Brown, *Biology and Society*, McGraw-Hill, 1976, p. 99.)

Categorization

Much of science is concerned with distinguishing kinds of things—the various categories and subcategories into which the substance of science is divided or grouped. There are metals versus nonmetals, organic versus nonorganic matter, flora versus fauna, vertebrates versus invertebrates, etc. No matter what the case, science writers use facts to distinguish between and, therefore, categorize the elements within a subject.

In dealing with vertebrates, for example, five categories are distinguished: mammals, birds, reptiles, amphibians, and fishes. For each group described, characteristics are given that indicate how they are alike so that all can be classified as vertebrates and yet distinguished from one another. In categorizing birds and amphibians, as shown in Example 11.5, each type is described and subdivided within its own class, yet its functions are compared with similar ones in another class. In taking

EXAMPLE

11.5

Birds. Birds are "feathered reptiles." Both birds and mammals are descended from reptiles, but they are descended from different groups of extinct reptiles. In fact, birds are descended from the earliest dinosaurs! Just as the hair of mammals is thought to have evolved from scales, the feathers of birds are thought to have evolved from scales. Birds still have scales on their legs. Most birds can be distinguished from reptiles because they are warm-blooded and can fly: however, some birds, like the ostrich (Fig. 6-24) cannot fly, and some lizards (Fig. 6-25) and snakes can glide. Some birds which seem to be flightless, the penguins, for example, "fly" underwater. Birds, like most reptiles, lay eggs: unlike most reptiles, however, they usually take care of their eggs and young. Most birds keep their eggs warm by sitting on them, and many carry food to the young after they have hatched. There are about 8200 species of birds, of which about 650 live in North America.

Amphibians. The mammals, reptiles, and birds that lay eggs usually do not lay them in water. Tough shells keep the eggs from drying out and protect them from other environmental hazards. Amphibians lay eggs, without tough shells, in water or in damp places. Young amphibians develop in water, undergoing metamorphosis to become adults (Fig. 6-26). Frogs, toads, and salamanders are the best-known amphibians (Fig. 6-27). Adult amphibians absorb oxygen and give off carbon dioxide in part through their skin, which must remain continually moist. Therefore, amphibian adults normally live in or near water, and very often are active only at night because they are less likely to dry out at night than in the daytime. There are about 2000 known species of amphibians.

(*Source:* P. R. Ehrlich, R. W. Holm, and I. Brown, *Biology and Society*, McGraw-Hill, 1976, p. 169.)

notes, either in outline form or in an organizational table, make sure to note the distinguishing features of each major group of vertebrates and how they are similar and dissimilar.

Problems and Experiments

Scientists are always dealing with problems. They perform experiments, studies, and tests under controlled conditions and then attempt to observe results and formulate conclusions. When you read about a scientific problem in your text, and the scientist who tried to solve the problem, keep a few things in mind. First of all, the scientist made an observation from nature or from another experiment which was either puzzling or intriguing. In order to find some logic behind the observation, the scientist did some experimenting and some observing, which resulted in either a successful answer or further questions. In the case of a success, the results become laws or rules, or phenomena are labeled. As you read about a problem and the way a scientist tried to solve it, ask yourself the following questions:

- What did the scientist observe that caused questions to be raised?

- Did the scientist state a hypothesis or project thoughts about the phenomena?

- What experiments did the scientist perform to try to prove or disprove the hypothesis?

- What did the scientist observe as a result of the experiments that proved or disproved the original observation or hypothesis?

- Can the results be stated in terms of scientific rules or laws?

A good set of notes taken from reading about scientific problems and experiments should reflect the answers to these questions.

A FURTHER WORD ABOUT SCIENCE STUDY TECHNIQUES

Most science courses also have lab sections. These are class hours devoted to working through experiments in a lab setting. They are as common in the life sciences as in the physical sciences. Biology, botany, and zoology labs, for example, are usually concerned with examining, probing, and comparing the various organisms discussed in the lecture. On the other hand, physical science labs are usually concerned with experiments that graphically demonstrate the natural phenomena discussed in lectures. In many schools, lab hours are required but not included in the scheduled program. In other words, you have to fit them into your schedule yourself. This is especially true of biology labs and labs associated with medical and dental programs. If this is the case for you, be sure to set aside a specific time and attend labs regularly. Leaving two, three, or more labs to do at once requires large chunks of time that you can't afford to give all at once, especially when midquarters or final exams are near.

If you have never had a lab course, relax. They are neither tough nor scary. Like everything else, they require systematic thought and action, resulting in your being in control of the situation.

Let's make the analogy between a lab course and either cooking a family dish or doing a construction project. In either case, familiarity with the steps in the process of cooking or construction is necessary before you begin. In addition, you must check to see whether you have all the proper tools and ingredients and make sure you know their names and where to locate them in the kitchen or work area. In some cases, there may be photos of what the task or project will look like on completion or during the various phases of preparation. If not, you can use your imagination, perhaps basing the mental picture on some previous similar experience. Beginning to get the idea?

If you have not had a lab course before, go to the lab to which you have been assigned and check it out. How is it set up? Where are the various pieces of equipment located in the room? What are the various pieces of equipment and how do they work? Either an instructor or a lab assistant will be glad to demonstrate them to you.

Before you attend the first lab session, become familiar with the lab manual. Preview it as you would any other text. Also preview the particular experiment to be done during the class. As in the case of a recipe or other direction, read it in its entirety. Get an overall view of what it is about. Ask yourself some questions. Visualize yourself in the lab. What is the purpose of the experiment? In general, what will you be required to do and what equipment will you be required to use? When it is completed, what should you see as the end result?

When you complete the general reading, go back and reread the experiment slowly, step by step, visualizing yourself in the lab setting performing each of the steps in turn. The idea is to go to the lab so well-rehearsed that it will be like working with an old familiar recipe or construction project.

Lab results usually must be written up in the lab manual. This means recording your observations for each step in the process. Needless to say, these observations have to be accurate and neat. Rehearsing the steps in the process will allow you to feel comfortable and relaxed about the work. You can then leave your mind open to anticipate the results. Many students who go to a lab unprepared panic when the unexpected happens. They are more concerned with the process than the results, and so they do not know whether what is happening is correct.

Write your lab results neatly and accurately as soon after the lab class as possible.

In summary, in order to become familiar with the lab:

- Read the lab experiment twice—once for general comprehension of the purpose and process of the experiment, the second time slowly and carefully to learn the step-by-step procedure for what you will be doing in the lab.

- Work at the lab experiment patiently and systematically, anticipating the results.

- Write up your lab observations accurately and neatly immediately after the lab.

Problems

Many of the physical sciences have problems at the end of each chapter or in a separate book of problems accompanying the text. Like any other type of problem solving, physical science problems should not (and mostly cannot) be worked until you understand the content of the chapter. It is also a good idea to record a completed sample of each type of problem in your lecture notes. Chemistry formulas, like algebraic equations, are learned best when you put them on flash cards as you meet them in your work and then recite and review them frequently. Work and rework problems in science just as you would in a math course. Work from different unknowns. You may have been taught to convert atoms to moles in chemistry, and therefore you know how to make all the proper substitutions, but on the test you may be asked to reverse the process. The few minutes of panic you experience can greatly influence your final test score. If you practice solving the problem by going from one unknown to another, you can avoid this difficulty.

Exams

Science exams cover the content of the course. Therefore, you will have to know vocabulary, facts, causes, effects, categories, and processes. Following the general rules of test preparation, including spacing practice, organizing the material, and anticipating and reciting the answers to potential test questions, is essential. Science tests call for knowing the facts, but questions requiring application of these facts to other scientific events, real or imagined, are just as prevalent. It is very important to keep this in mind when you study. Students in dietetic, nursing, or dental programs, for example, will constantly find themselves being asked to apply the facts to hypothetical medical situations. Students taking science courses for distribution requirements can use the examples and case studies from the text or lecture to aid in prediction of application-type questions.

SUMMARY

— Science courses are divided into two categories. The life sciences are concerned with living things, and the physical sciences with the elements of the physical world in which we live.

— Study techniques for the sciences include time-planning, adequate preparation for lectures, and a systematic approach to text study.

— Learn the scientific vocabulary as soon as possible in order to understand both the lecture and the text.

— Science writing consists of some fairly regular patterns used to explain the content. These include using facts to explain and illustrate definitions, explain processes, and show cause and effect relationships. Much of science is also categorized, showing how two or more things in the same group or different groups are similar or dissimilar.

— Science labs require special attention and preparation before the class in order to ensure good results. After the lab, notes on observations should be written immediately, accurately, and neatly.

— Science is concerned with questions. A large part of science study should revolve around the questioning techniques described earlier in this book.

STUDYING MATH | 12

This chapter is concerned with math study techniques. It gives background information on the subject, specifically on the cumulative nature of math and the problems associated with a poor math background. It goes on to discuss both basic and specific study techniques for math, including problem solving. It ends with a section on math anxiety and an assessment quiz to check your basic math ability.

Mentally review your experiences and attitudes toward the subject of math.

My experiences with math have been _____

_____

_____

_____

My attitude toward math is _____

_____

_____

_____

Therefore, in reading this chapter, the information you will want to pay particular attention to concerns _____

_____

_____

_____

Few subjects strike so much terror into many students' hearts and minds than math. Math shows up in either pure or applied form in almost every curriculum; it is required or recommended for programs in such diverse areas as drafting, nursing, accounting, psychology, social work, the sciences, and even music. Although math is used in some form every day, from balancing a checkbook to working with recipes or in estimating the miles per gallon a car is getting, in a formal classroom setting math becomes an obstacle to progress. More about this in the section on math anxiety.

BACKGROUND INFORMATION ON MATH

Math is a cumulative subject. Everything that you learn is dependent on what went before it. From the simplest to the more difficult, it all builds like blocks. We all began by learning what "how many" meant. Once we knew that 5 meant a certain number of fingers, then 5 more were added. If you knew the idea 10, then when 5 was taken away, you knew you were back to 5, and so forth. The school curriculum was based on an additive principle: first learn numbers, then how to add them, then how to subtract them, then multiplication, and so on. Day by day, the blocks were added to form the structure we know as math.

Since math is cumulative, the courses you are now taking have their bases in material you learned as far back as elementary school. For example, students in nursing courses must use such fundamental concepts as ratio and proportion to work out solutions to dosage and intravenous drug problems. In business statistics, students use their knowledge of equations and word problems that began in junior and senior high school. Naturally, the knowledge of one math course is essential to every one that follows it in a sequence.

One pitfall to success in math is a weak background in the fundamentals—an inadequate knowledge of such functions as fractions, decimals, percents, ratios, proportions, equations, and word problems. The brief assessment at the end of the chapter may help you determine any of your weak areas. Most learning labs also have such diagnostic material as well as math review material.

If you feel your entire background is weak, before you take any math classes, it would be a good idea to review the subject on your own. Use materials from the learning center or from any basic math review book in the library.

If you are in a math class now and recognize a weak point, remedy it immediately with the help of the instructor, by reading a basic math book in your area of weakness, or from the learning lab personnel. More about this in the section on math anxiety.

BASIC STUDY TECHNIQUES FOR MATH

Many of the basic study techniques discussed earlier in this book are as applicable to math as to any other subject.

It is important to do math on a daily basis. Skipping your assignments for even one day means expending twice the effort the next day. If you are unsure how to work the problems today, tomorrow's assignment will be all the more difficult because it is partially based on the previous work. Most students find it beneficial to do math assignments in the first free hour after math class, while the principles are still fresh in their minds. As is the case with other subjects, in any math class with a lecture, it's a good idea to go over the notes before tackling the book or the problems.

In many college classes, math is done almost independently. Since many math texts are programmed, the student is responsible for working a chapter and then taking a math quiz on the material in a math lab. Getting behind means skipping that daily test. When too many daily tests are missed, the midterm and final exams become very difficult. Basically, it's up to you. But that is true of math classes with lectures, too. The instructor speaks to and demonstrates a point and then assigns problems which give practice in the concept discussed. The instructor is really not interested in collecting the problems for grading. That's your responsibility. The important test is the one given in class, which is corrected and graded to see whether you understood the topic.

Some students find it helpful to schedule long blocks of time for math; others tire easily and like to work at it in several short study sessions. Do whichever suits you and contributes to your success as a math student.

In a math lecture class, pay more attention to the lecturer than to your notes. It is more important to follow the drift of the lecture and learn the concept being explained and demonstrated than it is to have a "complete" set of notes. Math notes should generally reflect large ideas and ideally a completed problem as a model for use as a study guide.

Since most math teachers follow the text pretty closely, another way to take notes is to read the text before going to class. Note the points you don't understand and want to hear in class. If you don't hear them or still don't understand them when you do hear them, raise your hand and ask a question. The odds are that several other people in the class had the same question but weren't brave enough to ask it. When you feel comfortable with a previously misunderstood point, write some notes in the textbook to help you later.

Editing notes after class is important. Remember the illustration on page 68 in Chapter 4 on listening and note-taking. It was recommended that you edit math notes by putting the formulas, problems, etc., in neat, completed form on the back of the previous page.

Math, like every other subject, must be reviewed and recited. In courses with formulas, proofs, or theorems, it's a good idea to put each one on a flash card and carry the cards around for quick and frequent study. Make them for each chapter as you read it rather than waiting till just before an exam.

If you keep your work up to date, getting ready for a math exam becomes a matter of reviewing as many problems as you can. One word of caution. There is more than one way to state a problem or see what you know. Math tests are application tests. An instructor may have shown you how to solve an equation when the unknown was on the right side of the equation. On the test, the same equation may show up with the unknown on the left side. That means reversing some of the processes. If you haven't done the problem in a variety of ways when studying, seeing it for the first time on the test can be mind-boggling. When you work sample problems for a test, work them in a variety of ways.

SPECIAL STUDY TECHNIQUES

There are two special techniques associated with studying math. One is reading a math textbook; the other is problem solving.

Reading a Math Text

Reading a math text is a slow, laborious task. For one thing, it is different from almost all other reading, since it is complicated by the combination of words and symbols interlaced with examples.

The purpose behind reading a math text is to get the idea being put across, to understand the whys and hows of the process, and ultimately to work the problems, proving by application that you understand the concept completely and thoroughly. The concept is usually presented in a series of words and an accompanying diagram or example. Reading occurs one step at a time. Read a sentence or two and then observe its application in the example. The process is repeated over and over, alternating reading the text with discovering how and why the problem exemplifies the process described. The end result is that you not only can verbalize the process, you know why the mathematical operation is being done. It is only after you have this understanding that you can work the problems.

Some of the techniques described in Chapter 5 for text reading also apply to math reading. It is a good idea to preview the section before you read it slowly to get a general idea of what it is about. Read with a pencil in your hand, making notes in the book that will aid you in your understanding and ultimately in problem solving. Recite and review the concept, the process, and any definitions. Although memory is important, a thorough understanding of the process, and its subsequent application to problems, is the real aim in studying math.

A big factor in reading math is the brief language which explains a complicated idea. Math writing is thrifty, with a few words standing for a lot of information. This means that math vocabulary is very precise, with each word standing for an idea that was explained in a previous lesson.

Most new vocabulary words are carefully defined in the text. They are usually accompanied by an illustration or example. For example, different geometric shapes, such as trapezoids and rhomboids, may be defined and described, but a picture of each accompanies the words.

As in science, there are many old, familiar words which have special math meanings. The word "product" means a "commodity," or something that is manufactured, sold, or bought. In math, it is the result of multiplying numbers together.

Another factor in math language is that symbols or pictures stand for words and ideas. They have to be known and understood in order for your reading to make sense. This goes for signs representing basic operations, such as $+, -, \times,$ and $\div$, as well as symbols that convey a meaning, such as $>$ (is greater than) or $<$ (is less than).

Problem Solving

Reading problems in math is not unlike other text-reading assignments in that you have to know what the problem in saying or, more precisely, asking. In other text reading you ask yourself, What did it say? In reading math problems you ask yourself the same question. To find the answer to that question, read the problem completely. Then go back and read it part by part until you understand all the information you have been given. You should be able to put it in your own words, much as you would with any other reading. Once you can state what the problem is saying, isolate all the information that is important. Determine which operations, formulas, and procedures you will use, and then go ahead and solve it. It's a good idea to check your results by substituting the answer in the unknown spot. Let's go through the procedure on a basic interest problem.

1. Read the Problem
   Problem: Ms. Jones had a savings account in a local bank. At the end of the year she stopped by to have the interest on her $500 account figured. The bank is paying 6 percent per year. How much interest did she get?

2. State it in your own words: _____

   _____

   _____

3. What information have you been given? _____

   _____

4. What procedure or formula will you use? _____

_____

5. Solve the problem.

6. Check the results.

Let's go over the results. Your responses may be slightly different from the following ones, but don't worry about that as long as your answers reflect the same ideas.

Put in simple words, the problem says:

- Given a $500 savings account, how much interest will it earn at the end of one year if the annual rate is 6 percent?

You are given the following facts:

- The savings account balance is $500.

- The time period is one year.

- The rate of interest is 6 percent per year.

- There is a lot of extraneous information that you do not need to understand or solve the problem: the account holder's name, the fact that the account was in a local bank, and the fact that she stopped by to have the interest entered in her passbook.

Since the problem is asking for the amount of interest paid, you would use the simple interest formula $I = prt$, where I = interest, p = principal, r = rate of interest, and t = time or number of years. The process implied by the formula is this: I, or interest, will be obtained by multiplying $p \times r \times t$, or principal times rate times time.

$I = prt$
$I = \$500 \times .06 \times 1$
$I = \$30.00$

Check it. $30 = 500 \times .06 \times 1$

Now you do another one:

1. Read the Problem
   Problem: John borrowed $7500 from his bank to buy a new car. He wants to repay the loan over the next three years because he doesn't

want to extend his indebtedness any longer than that. The bank charges 9 percent a year. How much interest will he pay per year? For the three years?

2. State it in your own words. _____

_____

_____

3. What information have you been given? _____

_____

_____

4. What procedure or formula will you use? _____

_____

5. Solve the problem.

6. Check the results.

Remember to use these steps in solving math problems.
Answer to problem:
    John will pay $675 interest for one year, $2025 for three years.

MATH ANXIETY

What are your reactions to the word "math"? For many people, the associations are mostly negative. As we said earlier, math is one of the most widely avoided subjects in the college curriculum.

Both men and women (but especially women) tend to take as few math classes as possible. This has several implications. One is that most Americans know less math than they are capable of learning. A second is that the average American relies on others and has to trust them to figure out the mathematical sides of life, such as preparing income tax forms or figuring out the discount on sale items and interest charges. A third implication is that this lack of knowledge places limitations on job options and therefore on the earning capacity of many people, especially women.

Why the great avoidance? For many it is a reaction against bad experiences in classes going as far back as elementary school. Such things as being ridiculed by peers for asking dumb questions or the insistence by teachers on accuracy and the need to give the "one and only correct answer" to a problem turns many students off to math. For others, it's a reaction to attitudes or opinions they hear expressed by family or friends: "What's the sense of learning this? We'll never use it again, anyway."

If you feel that you have a poor attitude toward math, can you trace the reasoning behind your thinking? _____

What experiences have you had to make you math-shy? _____

Listen to yourself the next time you have to take a math class or when you are doing math homework. Chances are, you are saying things like:

"I'm not good at math."

"Boy, I have a lot of math homework."

"I hope I'll do the problems OK."

"But I probably can't because I'm not good at math."

If you think that's going around in verbal circles, you're right!

Let's examine this a little more closely. First of all, the circle began with a negative statement that also implies a poor self-concept: "I'm not good at math." If you say you're not good at it and can't do it, the odds are that you won't. You seem to have made an irreversible mental decision. If you say you won't do math, this implies that you choose not to do it and are willing to suffer the consequences of your actions. This is followed by a statement of fact: "I have a lot of math homework." If you're not good at it and can't do math, how are you going to do the homework? Your attitude affects your mind set, which affects your concentration on the task at hand—doing math homework. You follow up the statement of fact with a statement of wish fulfillment: "I hope I'll be able to do the problems OK." Unfortunately, wishing never made anything so, and at about this time the round-about reasoning comes full circle when you say, "But I probably can't because I'm not good at math.."

The circle must be broken between the "hoping" and the "probably can't." Instead of hoping, you will have to do something about your math skills to break the math anxiety circle.

HOW TO BREAK THE MATH ANXIETY CHAIN

Step 1: Build Up Your Basic Math Background
The odds are that if you are having trouble with math, your math background is not as good as it could be. Since math is cumulative, with one set of skills and knowledge dependent on what preceded it, a general

review of the basics is usually helpful. Many schools have a general math refresher course that is very valuable, especially for those who haven't had math in a long time and have self-doubts about going on to more. Many schools with learning centers stock programmed math review books that begin with the basics. Either a course or an individual program designed to meet your particular needs will help you overcome a weak background. Such courses or programs usually begin with a test that covers basic math, such as the elementary functions of adding, subtracting, multiplying, and dividing, as well as fractions, decimals, word problems, and weights and measurements. From this, you can discover your strengths and weaknesses and work on improving your background.

Step 2: Talk About It
Like last year's fashions hidden in closets, problems not discussed tend to stay in the dark and grow more outdated and difficult to deal with as time goes by.

If you are experiencing (or expect to experience) any degree of math insecurity, talk to your instructor. There are many things you and the instructor can do to help with the problem. The instructor may be able to recommend another book that has a better explanation of the concept with which you are having difficulty, get you in touch with a tutor or another student for assistance, or

- Give you a further clarification or explanation of the problem or concept.

- Put you in touch with your college learning center and some tutorial assistance (if your school has such a program) as well as help with study and test-taking skills for math.

- Relax the time constraints on a test or two. Frequently, students say they knew the work but panicked while being tested, only to have the knowledge come back after the test. Testing under untimed conditions helps relieve the pressure. Once a student does well on an untimed math test, the renewed confidence can be used on timed tests.

- Put you in touch with a math anxiety program in or near your city. These programs are becoming more prevalent. They are meant to help students overcome long-standing math anxiety by teaching math skills, relaxation, study skills, and sharing of the problem with other students experiencing the same problem.

Step 3: Learn to Use Relaxation Techniques
The section on anxiety in test taking on pages 145–151 described the use of relaxation techniques for overcoming general test panic.

These techniques are just as valid for math anxiety. If you haven't read that section yet, go back and do so now, making the application to math.

A BRIEF BASIC MATH ASSESSMENT

A brief math ability assessment follows. In each of the basic categories, there are problems to check your level of skill. Obviously, the assessment is not complete or scientifically validated. It is just a way for you to examine your skills. Use the results to locate the areas in which you are sure of your math skills, the areas in which you are experiencing difficulty or uncertainty as to how to complete the mathematical process, and the areas in which your ability and knowledge is inadequate. Read steps 1 and 2. Then return to these directions and begin again at step 3.

Before you begin, how do you feel about taking this assessment?

I feel _____

_____

Step 1. Work the problems in each section of the assessment.
Step 2. Check your answers against the correct ones that follow the assessment.
Step 3. Circle the answer to each problem that you did not get correct.
Step 4. Assess yourself.

In which categories did you have errors?

Whole numbers _____   Equations _____

Fractions _____   Ratios _____

Decimals _____   Proportions _____

Percents _____

What types of errors did you make?

Did you not have knowledge of the process? _____

Did you not know basic math facts? _____

Did you make silly calculation errors? _____

What do you feel would be the best way to improve your basic math skills?

Take a course _____   Work on your own _____

Don't know, and so I'll discuss it with an instructor _____

the learning lab people _____   a counselor _____

For what reasons do you feel it is important to improve your math skills?

I have to take more math courses _____

It will help in the courses I have to take in the future _____

For my own personal satisfaction _____

ASSESSING YOUR BASIC MATH ABILITY

1. Whole Numbers

Add

A. 2603
   1979

B. 4792
   8314
   7999

C. 8305
    902
     87
   6431
   3500

Subtract

A. 3765
   1432

B. 7842
   6959

C. 3007
   1509

Multiply

A.   136
     92

B. 4876
    653

C. 4070
     305

Divide

A. $7\overline{)35749}$

B. $35\overline{)126059}$

C. $305\overline{)629876}$

2. Fractions

Add and simplify where possible

A. 4 1/12
   6 7/12
   9 3/12

B. 3 1/4
   7 1/8
   1 5/6

C. 6/9
   4/9
   2/9

D.   5/6
     2/3
   6

Subtract

A. 18/49
   12/49

B. 12/4
    9/8

C. 12 4/5
     1/4

D. 8
     3/8

Multiply

A. 1/8 × 1/8

B. 5/12 × 1/3

C. 9 × 5/7

D. 8 × 3 3/5

Divide

A. 3/4 ÷ 1/8

B. 26 ÷ 4/9

C. 4 1/2 ÷ 18

3. Decimals

Add   72.9 + 3.9 + 12.160 + 936.9

Subtract   31.92
        8.09

Multiply   1.97
        12.9

Divide
A. $8\overline{).56}$ B. $12\overline{)14.4}$ C. $75\overline{)1.6000}$

4. Percents

Change the following fractions to percents
A. 1/2   B. 3/10   C. 5/12   D. 5/8

Change the following decimals to percents
A. .10   B. .07   C. .5

Find 25 percent of 600

Problem 1
Ms. X bought a dress for $42.00 This was 25 percent off the original price. What was the original price?

Problem 2
Mr. Y bought a car stereo for $500. When he turned it in for a new one, he got $100. What percent did he lose?

5. Equations, Ratios, and Proportions

Solve the following equations:
A. $6X + 3 = 18$ B. $5X - 6 = 2X + 1$
C.   Bill and Joe want to buy a stereo together. They have a total of $300. Bill has $125 more than 3X as much as Joe. How much does each have?

Do the following ratio problems:
D.   Three friends have a total of $240, and the amount is in the ratio of 1 to 2 to 3. How much does each have?

Proportions
E.   Find the missing term $4:15 = 8 = X$
F.   Solve $\dfrac{3X}{9} = \dfrac{5}{4}$
G.   Z can jog 6 miles in two hours. How far can he jog at the same rate in five hours?

ANSWERS TO BASIC MATH ABILITY ASSESSMENT

1. Whole numbers
Add
A. 4582   B. 21105   C. 19225

Subtract
A. 2333   B.   883   C.   1498

Multiply
A. 12512   B. 3184028   C. 1241350

Divide
A. 5107   B. 3601 11/35r   C. 2065 51/305r

2. Fractions
Add
A. 19 11/12   B. 12 5/24   C. 1 1/3   D. 7 1/2

Subtract
A. 6/49   B. 3/8   C. 12 11/20   D. 7 5/8

Multiply
A. 1/64   B. 5/36   C. 6 3/7   D. 28 4/5

Divide
A. 6   B. 76   C. 1/4

3. Decimals
Add   1025.860

Subtract   4.898

Multiply   28.3928

Divide   A. 7   B. .95   C. 1021 1/3

4. Percents
Changing fractions to percents
A. 50%   B. 30%   C. 21.6%   D. 62.5%

Changing decimals to percents
A. 10%   B. 7%   C. 50%
25% of $600 = $150

Problem 1 $56

Problem 2   80%

5. Equations, Ratios, and Proportions

A. 2 1/2   B. 2 2/3   C. Joe — 43.75
                                    Bill—256.25
D. Friend 1 has $40, friend 2 has $80, and friend 3 has $120
E. 30
F. 3 3/4
G. 15

SUMMARY

— Although math is a subject dealt with every day, it is consciously avoided by many students.

— Math is cumulative and must be worked on daily. One concept follows another and, therefore, must be understood before you go on to the next one.

— Some of the basic study techniques discussed earlier in this book are just as applicable to math or any other subject. For example, spaced practice, careful reading, editing lecture notes, reciting, and reviewing.

— Math does have special study techniques. Reading math is unlike most other kinds of reading because of the abbreviated language and the use of symbols that stand for words.

— Use the series of steps set out to help in problem solving to understand the nature of the problem and how to solve it.

— Math anxiety is a common complaint among college students, especially women. You can reduce anxiety by improving your background, getting help, talking about the problem to others, using relaxation techniques, or joining a math anxiety group.

IV | A FEW FINAL WORDS AND AN ASSESSMENT

CONCENTRATING ON THE TASK | 13

This chapter is concerned with concentration—paying attention to the task at hand in order to get it done in the most efficient, effective way possible. It discusses some of the reasons behind poor concentration habits, including procrastination, personal concerns, self-image, uncertainty over or lack of a career goal, lack of a place of study, and lack of a purpose for each study session.

Mentally review your ability to stick to and concentrate on a task. When you can't concentrate, what verbal statements keep going through your mind? Which of the following areas are they concerned with?

Procrastinating _____   Personal concerns _____

Career goals   _____   Self-image   _____

How do you feel your study place helps or hinders your ability to

concentrate? _____

_____

_____

Do you usually have a purpose for each study session (other than reading

till you come to the end of the assignment)? Yes? _____ No? _____

Therefore, based on the answers you gave to the questions above, you will want to pay particular attention to the following information in this

chapter _____

_____

_____

Do you ever hear yourself saying, "I'll do that later"? Do you cut class for no good reason? Do you dislike the courses you are taking? Do you find excuses for not studying? Do you jump up from the desk and find lots of things to do instead of hitting your books? Do you daydream during lectures? If you answered yes to even one of these questions, the odds are that you probably have difficulty concentrating on schoolwork.

Everyone at one time or another has trouble concentrating on the task at hand or getting motivated to attack a new job, problem, or study assignment. Concentration requires discipline, and discipline is difficult to acquire and maintain.

Let's look into the meaning behind the answers to these questions and consider some common causes of poor concentration.

CAUSES OF POOR CONCENTRATION

Procrastination

Do you put off doing assignments? Household chores? Personal goals? Is school the only thing about which you procrastinate? If you answered yes to the first set of questions and no to the second question, you probably tend to put off most things, whether they are related to school, personal goals, or your relations with other people. Procrastination seems to be a way of life rather than a sometime thing for a lot of people.

There is no one answer to the question of why people procrastinate. Putting things off is a defense mechanism for students who want to succeed without really trying or for students who have unrealistic expectations of themselves or are afraid to try hard at something because they have gotten poor results from previous efforts. Yet again, some procrastinate to get even with the adult world, mainly parents, the boss, a teacher, or some other authority figure. There are probably as many reasons as there are procrastinators. Generally speaking, procrastination is a self-defeating behavior. It holds us up from completing tasks or attempting new ones. It results in a feeling of anxiety. It usually means that we make a lot of self-putdown statements about our abilities, appearance, or social skills. Sometimes it even results in our affecting the lives of others negatively.

Everyone delays tasks, reorders priorities, and sets new goals. If you accomplish what you set out to do or make up your mind that a task can be put off without harm to yourself, you are probably not procrastinating. However, if you put things off or complete them at the last minute or after the deadline, all the while berating yourself for doing so, you are probably procrastinating.

What do you say to yourself when you put things off? "I can do it later!" "It's really not that important anyway!" "I'd rather go with the crew than stay home and study!" "If I don't go, maybe they'll never call and ask me to go with them again!" Do any of these sound familiar?

How do you feel physically when you put things off? Anxious, perhaps even a bit nervous?

Our minds and bodies give us messages. The verbal messages usually reflect rationalizations for our behavior—reasons why we think it is okay to delay studying. The physical messages usually reflect the body's awareness of one's mental state.

What tends to happen is that we wind up enjoying neither event—the one we do as a substitute for studying or the studying itself. While you procrastinate, the mind is thinking about studying; and while you study, your mind is berating you for procrastinating. It's a no win situation.

Self-Image

Everyone has an image of himself or herself as a student. The picture usually comes from messages, both verbal and nonverbal, given by parents, peers, teachers, or the educational system, or from the values of society in general.

Positive messages usually reflect ideas of personal competence, support for striving and learning, and the value of an education. Negative messages usually reflect ideas of incompetence such as being a troublemaker or questioning the value of studying hard to get an education in order to succeed.

Some students report that they had to bring home good grades but were never questioned about what they had learned. Others say friends had a heavy influence on their attitudes toward school and learning. In either case, now that they are in college, studying in general and concentrating in particular are difficult. Without a real idea of their ability, and sometimes with a weak background in many basic areas, they are forced to confront themselves as students for the first time. It becomes easy to slip into old behavior patterns, studying at the last minute or grabbing the pleasure of friends' company, before doing the work of school and learning.

Our society and even our families talk about the value of an education. Yet many college graduates are in less than professional jobs. It's a discouragement that leads many to ask, "What am I doing here at this desk?" There goes concentration.

If a former not-too-interested student decides to change and become an interested student at college, he or she runs the risk of ridicule from friends. One young woman I know very innocently began explaining an algebra problem to a friend who complained she couldn't get the work being done in class. The reply was not "Thank you" or "Now I get it," but "Since when did you get so smart and start studying?" It's hard to break an old image people have of you. Always thought of as a fun person, this student had to come to terms with her friend's image of her and her own abilities and attitudes toward school and learning.

Many women have to break the stereotype of not having to be bright, especially in science and math. Although women are in the majority in most schools, they drop out earlier than men, take less math and science, and pursue less prestigious careers, mostly because of the image they have of themselves as students.

How do you picture yourself as a student?

_____

_____

What messages did you get from your parents, teachers, and peers regarding your competence as a student? grades? learning? the value of an education?

_____

_____

How would you like to picture yourself as a student?

_____

_____

What would you have to do to attain your goal?

_____

_____

Lack of Academic or Career Goals

For some students, procrastination related to school is closely associated with having little or no idea of an academic major or career and life goals. They've drifted into college because they had to go somewhere after high school, or after several years of nonrewarding work or being at home. School seemed like the place to go as a start on finding a new career. Going through the daily routine of classes and homework, they may be questioning the reason for being in school and the necessity for studying specific subjects. Concentrating on reading a text or writing a paper is difficult with these internal noises running around in your head.

Having a purpose is important for concentration. Sometimes a purpose does not have a tangible reward—something you can see or something you get from someone else. You have to set your own purpose, and the reward is something you give yourself for an accomplishment that makes you proud. Taking a required course in English grammar or math, for example, serves a purpose in your life and does, believe it or not, carry a reward. While you may never spend time solving algebraic equations, you will learn problem-solving techniques and discipline that carry over into other areas of your life. You may never write the great American novel, but writing a literate letter of consumer protest or praise does have its rewards when you get action or help solving a community or personal problem.

Course sampling is sometimes necessary in order to find an academic major. By not setting a purpose or motivating yourself to do your best, you lessen your chances of success in the course in particular, and school in general.

Many schools offer career education courses. While they will not supply the answer to your career dilemma, they will help you find out more about your interests, skills, and values and help you find the occupational information necessary for making intelligent and informed career choices.

Lack of a Place to Study

Where you study plays an important role in how well you concentrate. We tend to make associations between a place and the activity we do there. If you sit in the same chair to study and to watch television, the odds are pretty good that you'll keep looking up at the tube or think about TV even while it's turned off. If you sit on your bed with a textbook, you'll very likely fall asleep. The association between the bed and sleep is too strong for any textbook to win out or for you to concentrate while sitting or lying there.

If you study in the student lounge or eating area, you are really asking for someone to come along and interrupt you—to take you away from the task at hand, in other words, your books.

If you study at home, especially if the other inhabitants are not students, you may be interrupted frequently by requests to run errands or do chores. Nonstudents usually have difficulty figuring out why the student is not always available and needs quiet time to get studying done.

If you go home early in the day to an empty house, it is always a temptation to do other things, to take a nap or flip on the TV set just for a while.

If it sounds like every place is a pitfall, full of temptations, that's probably true, especially if you are having trouble concentrating.

The best places are fairly quiet although not completely silent, have good light and suitable study furniture, are neither too hot nor too cold, and have other people around who are also silently busy. If it sounds a lot like a library or other student study area, you're right.

Once you've found the ideal study place, get in the habit of going back there regularly so that you can establish a strong association between the place and study behavior: reading, taking notes, working problems, reciting, etc.

STUDY LOCATION QUESTIONNAIRE

List the places where you generally tend to study.

Place 1 _____

Place 2 _____

Place 3 _____
What are the problems associated with concentrating in each place?

Place 1 _____

Place 2 _____

Place 3 _____
Is there anything that makes concentration possible in each place?

Place 1 _____

Place 2 _____

Place 3 _____
Summarize what you found out about your study places.

_____

_____

Should you eliminate any of the three areas as a study location in the

future?   Yes? _____ No? _____ Which one(s)? _____
Should you consistently return to one or more of these places in the

future?   Yes? _____ No? _____ Which one(s)? _____
Name other places where it would be better for you to go to in order to concentrate.

Place 1 _____

Place 2 _____

Place 3 _____
What would make these place more preferable as study locations?

Place 1 _____

Place 2 _____

Place 3 _____
When will you go there to study? List the times you will study there and the work you will attempt to accomplish in a specific time period.

TIME   STUDY GOAL

_____

_____

_____

What rewards will you give yourself for successful completion of your study goal in this new location?

Rewards _____

_____

HAVING A PURPOSE FOR STUDYING

Closely associated with concentration is consistency of study place and having a clear goal for what you want to accomplish at each study session. You've already found information on time-planning in Chapter 3. When you go to that ideal study place, make sure you know what you are going to do when you get there. Concentration is helped by having a purpose for a study session. If you want to do ten pages of reading in the hour that you have, knowing your goal beforehand makes for a better attitude, a better student, and usually a more productive study session.

Two suggestions that go along with setting a purpose for a study session are varying the length of your study time and varying the study activity itself. For example, you will probably be able to spend more time at one sitting writing a paper than straight reading. In order not to get bored, you might alternate between the two activities, changing each hour. This is especially true if you have to spend many hours writing on any one day. Spending too many hours working at one task becomes tedious, especially if it is not one of your favorite subjects. Resentment toward your assignments and school frequently results in a loss of concentration.

PERSONAL CONCERNS

The ability to get in gear to study and concentrate is very often preempted by personal concerns—the normal problems most people have in the course of daily living.

Many students are concerned about money—the wherewithal to pay for tuition and rent, buy food and clothing, and maintain an auto to get to school and work. If you don't have a job, or have a low-paying one, you're probably concerned with having enough money. If you have a well-paying full-time job, your concern is probably not with money but with having enough time for work, school, and a social life.

If you live with your family or with roommates in a situation where no one else is a student, you may find demands being made upon your time to do errands and chores you have always done, or new ones, since you appear to have more free time as a college student than you did when you were in high school.

Young students are frequently concerned with personal and intimate relationships—the pressures exerted by non-school-going friends to socialize rather than study, whether to marry, or whether to have a sexual relationship.

It is also a time of breaking away from one's family, asserting independence, yet being caught in a bind of still living at home, and therefore, still being under some control by one's parents.

Adults who return to school, especially women, feel that they still must perform all the family tasks they have always done in addition to their studies. Husbands and children, used to having errands and chores performed for them, expect Mom to continue in the old roles of chauffeur, cook, baker par excellence, seamstress, laundress, gardener, and check balancer. What's worse, Mom feels guilty when she doesn't perform up to the old standard. She feels equally guilty for not putting in the amount of study time she believes is necessary for someone who has been out of school for a while. Quite a bind.

What it comes down to is the inability or unwillingness to say no and the risk of displeasing others if you don't go along with the crowd or the family. It requires strength and determination to do it your own way. However, if school is a priority, it may require you to say no or "I'll be glad to do that for you after I study for my class (test)." A polite explanation goes a long way in helping your relationships with others. When you get caught up in being a people-pleaser, it usually results in suppressed anger (at yourself) and anxiety. When you finally get to study, your concentration suffers because the internally heard noises are louder than your study noises.

Well then, what can be done about these personal concerns?

If a problem has a solution, take care of whatever part of it you can before you begin to study. Make a call to set up a job interview, see your counselor about that job on campus, run the errand that needs doing. Small tasks that are completed are off your mind. Remember that these are tasks and not rewards, such as going to a movie, watching TV, or talking on the phone to a friend. Rewards come after your work is completed. Something pleasant to look forward to is a fine motivation, an aid to concentrating and accomplishing a purposeful and productive study session.

If a problem is big enough to cause mental distraction, you may have to forego studying until it is solved. This may mean lightening your course load, seeing your instructor or college counselor, or seeking professional help.

POOR STUDY HABITS

Another reason for concentration problems is poor study habits, but that's why you've read this book, isn't it?

SUMMARY

In summary, some things you can do for your image of yourself as a student and to improve your concentration include:

— Setting a definite time and place for study. The place should be quiet, clean, and uncluttered. The time should be well-planned and stuck to once you've set it aside for a specific task. Deadlines help get work done.

— Setting up a definite purpose for each study session, something specific you can measure as having accomplished once the time is up.

— Varying your study time to match your physical and emotional lows and peaks to your easiest and most difficult subjects. If a task is too big, break it down so you at least have a starting point.

— Varying your study activities, working longer on some tasks than on others.

— Learning to ask for help from others when you are stuck. It is impossible to concentrate if you are frustrated or lack information.

— Putting a task away for a while if you are fatigued or can't think. It's possible the answer may come to you later. If not, you can ask someone else for help.

— Planning time when you are unavailable to others, time you can use to study, think, daydream, or work on your future. The place as well as the time spent should make you inaccessible. Study or think in a place where you can't be interrupted by the phone. If you have to work near a phone, have someone else answer it and use a call-back system. That means setting aside time for phone calls rather than letting the phone own your time.

— Using rewards for work well done—a good study session followed by some socializing.

— Using rewards to accomplish work—studying your most favorite subject *after* studying the one you like the least.

— Realizing that concentration doesn't come in a box, bottle, or jar. To gain discipline, you have to work at it a little each day.

LOOKING BACKWARD AND FORWARD | 14

Now that you've come to the end of this book, whether you completed it on your own or as part of a study skills course, it is a good idea to reflect on both the content and yourself—what you have learned and how you intend to use it in the future.

The idea behind this book has been to provide you with study skills—the information and exercises to either make you aware of or reacquaint you with efficient, effective techniques for academic success.

It is hoped, therefore, that you have worked all the exercises and applied the study skills to your present academic needs. It is also hoped that you have given some thought to what skills you might need to use in future learning experiences, since it is assumed that education does not stop upon completion of a few courses for your own satisfaction or advancement or for a degree.

The following exercise is meant to get you to reflect on your learning needs, your learning experiences with this book, and your future use of what you have learned. Read the questions that follow, and answer them as completely as you can.

Answer for each.

—As you read and completed the exercises in each chapter, what were the five most important study skills areas about which you felt you needed information:

1. _____

_____

2. _____

_____

3. _____

_____

4. _____

_____

5. _____

_____

—For each area you listed above, write down the information you learned that you felt would help you.

1. _____

_____

2. _____

_____

3. _____

_____

4. _____

_____

5. _____

_____

—Which of the skills listed above have you actually applied to the courses you may be taking?

Skill _____   Course _____

Skill _____   Course _____

Skill _____   Course _____

Skill _____   Course _____

—Which ones did you find useful? _____

_____

_____

—Which ones did you not find useful? _____

_____

—What were the successful results of the skills you used and found
  helpful? _____

_____

—What problems did you encounter that kept what you tried from being
  useful? _____

_____

_____

—What do you feel you would need to do (if you want to turn it into a useful
  technique) to make it pay off and be a success? _____

_____

_____

—In what other study skills areas do you feel you still need help? ____

_____

_____

—Where would be the most likely place for you to get that assistance?

_____

_____

—Knowing what you do now about study skills, how would you begin (or
  what would you do) differently the next time you take classes? ____

_____

_____

—What did you learn about yourself as a student while reading this book?

_____

_____

—What did you learn about yourself as a person? _____

_____

_____

Good Luck!

INDEX